College Mentoring Handbook

The Way of the Self-Directed Learner

James L. Gray, Ed. D.

authorHOUSE®

AuthorHouse™
1663 Liberty Drive
Bloomington, IN 47403
www.authorhouse.com
Phone: 1 (800) 839-8640

Published by AuthorHouse 02/01/2017

ISBN: 978-1-5049-8151-4 (sc)
ISBN: 978-1-5049-8150-7 (e)

Library of Congress Control Number: 2016903111

Print information available on the last page.

Any people depicted in stock imagery provided by Thinkstock are models, and such images are being used for illustrative purposes only.
Certain stock imagery © Thinkstock.

This book is printed on acid-free paper.

Contents

The Mentoring Handbook is dedicated to the first-generation college students arriving on campuses today armed with passion and renewed hope for a bright future in a brave new world.

Foreword

The primary aim of this handbook is to introduce the college student—traditional or nontraditional—to a pragmatic approach focusing on applying useful strategies and tools to becoming an effectual self-directed learner in the twenty-first century and beyond. This handbook is not only designed to stimulate the interest of various types of college students in how they may exert themselves via the college experience for the global economy, but also to take the college students' learning goals and put them into transformative action during the actual learning process.

The journey to enroll in college today and the experience that the college student will have in the walls of the learning environment diverge sensationally from prior explanations for "why a college education" is so vital. Thus, in this handbook, the trending of a successful college student through the years of acquiring the college education and experience seemed not to necessarily portray a degree-seeking need, but it is predicated upon the following three essential tenets—purposeful learning, personal development, and self-directed learning.

For many years, the college experience has been about the same (or sustained relatively inconsequential changes): enroll, choose a major, manage expectations, purchase books and resource materials, attend the lectures, nurture collegiate relationships, perform assignments, take the tests, obtain the grades, graduate, go out and interview for a job, get hired, and pay back loans and other debts. However, this handbook could not have come at a better time than now, as it boosts the necessity of the college student to catch up with the current times through a hands-on mentoring resource book that provides a dose of empowerment and inspiration for the college as well as post-college real world awakenings. If the college is measuring up to preparing students for lasting and productive experiences or not, this college mentoring handbook is unwaveringly recommended as a guide for paradigm shift of the college student in becoming a successful self-directed learner.

The handbook features key mentoring lessons that can be easily followed (as a recipe) in any order, as preferred by the college student for guidance. Designed to stand alone, each lesson provides the college student an awesome growth experience.

At the onset of reading this handbook, the college student is encouraged to invest effort and time focusing on the factual stories contained in the mentoring lessons and, also, to reflect on impacts of the aforementioned tenets for the college engagement, experience, and exit to the real world.

John T. Wulu Jr., PhD
Associate professor (adjunct), University of Maryland University College; professor (adjunct), Montgomery College, Maryland

Preface

My insatiable passion to mentor college kids provides the starting point for writing the *Mentoring Handbook*. Concerned with what I came to view as a conventional or passive engagement approach to college, I wanted to offer students an alternative approach. What I came up with is what I later referred to as a self-directed learning approach, where students take personal responsibility for active learning, instead of being fed by faculty. Sadly, too many students are going off to college to engage in what I view as a traditional educational system that is passive in its approach to teaching.

The world has changed, but it does not seem, at least to me, that our education system has changed over the years to accommodate the new demands and realities brought about by a nascent global economy. Looking back, it's clear that the system has not made any notable structural changes from the time I started elementary school in the fall of 1949, nearly seven decades ago, to the present time. Students are merely viewed as empty vessels to be stuffed with information to prepare them for testing.

At the end of each school year, for the last five graduating classes, I have encountered students who are like lost balls in tall weeds. Interestingly enough, academic performance is never the issue. These kids graduate with GPAs well over 3.0 with degrees in marketable career fields but have no idea how to go about the business of looking for a job. In fact, many of them showed no signs of having significant work-ready skill sets. Of course, they won't say this is the case, but after a conversation with them it becomes apparent that they are passive learners. They absorbed the lectures, read the assigned books, and passed the exams. It is very much like Mark Twain remarked in a speech: "Students do not often (have) time get a good education because they let school get in the way." Listening to passive lectures and memorizing information solely for the purpose of getting good grades on exams is a prime example of school getting in the way of a good education.

For many students and parents, college can be a scary time. It is a life-changing event that brings new challenges, heightened responsibilities, and decision-making that will test the average student's academic and emotional capacity. My concern is that students are daunted by the mere thought of attending college. In the first place, most are not ready to engage in active learning requiring personal responsibility. Whatever advice and instructions they get is based on a traditional-passive classroom model. Based on the many conversations I've had with students, I would argue that many of them fail to make the postsecondary education learning experience a truly transformational consequence in their lives.

My personal mission in my post-retirement life is to empower students to change their view of college and how they see themselves engaging the college experience. I don't possess a magic wand or secret formula for success, but I do have a few ideas on a new mentoring conversation that I am confident will help students engineer a rewarding college experience that prepares them for transitioning into the labor market after graduating. My contention is, if students knew how to engage in self-directed learning, they would be motivated to do better. Hence, my thinking is to ignite a paradigm shift in the way students view the college experience simply by articulating a set of new engagement rules and strategies.

As my interest on this topic grew, my thoughts turned to writing a book to help minority students succeed in college. Success, from my point of view, was not just getting a degree and accumulating a high GPA. No! I viewed success in part on whether a student had built up relevant employability potential along with his/her degree. A big concern for me also was what I considered to be a failure on the part of students to understand their consumer-investor status in the education process at the college level—that is, not showing a level of personal responsibility comparable to the family investment. Student performance suggested to me that they were oblivious to the enormous cost of college and the extraordinary sacrifices their families were making to get them a college education. Hence, students settled on playing passive roles in their educational process, unaware that they had greater personal engagement responsibility in the learning environment. Somehow or another, they never got the memo on personal responsibility for learning when transitioning from high school to college.

Realizing how unaware and ill-informed students were concerning the need to engage in and take personal responsibility for interactive learning, *The College Mentoring Handbook: The Way of the Self-Directed Learner* seemed to have a timely message concerning the memo they did not get. Hereinafter referred to as the *Mentoring Handbook,* it introduces students to an entrepreneurial approach to college, giving them practical strategies and tools to help them succeed beyond earning a degree and high GPA. Ultimately, it is my hope that the *Mentoring Handbook* helps to prepare students to be highly competitive job seekers in today's ever-changing economic global landscape. It presents fresh information and ideas on (1) the importance of planning desired outcomes, (2) what is to be achieved from engaging in the college learning environment, (3) how to learn inside and outside the classroom, (4) vital educational and career products, (5) the importance of being a self-directed learner in a passive educational system, (6) the value in working with other students, and (7) engaging faculty in the role of educational consultants.

A conscious decision has been made to refrain from profiling iconic people as examples of success. My chief objective is to simply offer practical insights to students on how to make the most of the college experience considering the world they find themselves in today. I want to empower and inspire students, particularly African Americans, to see education as a powerful tool that they can use to create incredible life stories in a world that's undergoing extraordinary change and new possibilities.

The principles, concepts, and anecdotal information presented here were derived from countless conversations with acquaintances and associates, parents, high school and college students, college administrators, and leaders in the business community who indulged me as I picked their brains while sharing my idea for the *Mentoring Handbook*. My hope is that students read the *Mentoring Handbook*, implement what they read, and, in the process, follow the way of the self-directed learner and engineer a rewarding and productive college education—that is, not relying solely on classroom instructors to impart knowledge, focusing attention on building strong resumes and academic portfolios that appeal to prospective employers, managing and using time wisely, and seeking learning opportunities beyond the classroom.

Acknowledgments

This handbook was produced with the help of many people who supported my reason for writing it. They believed in its purpose and assisted me every step of the way. I am indebted to them for sharing their points of view, insights, and constructive criticism. Likewise, I am grateful to them for pushing me, particularly during the times when I questioned whether to keep going. For the family members who encouraged me to share my thoughts on ways parents can better help their kids succeed in college, I sincerely thank you.

Specifically, I must begin by saying a special and heartfelt thank you to my wife, Kathryn Gray, an educator for over four decades. Kathryn's poignant stories enhanced my understanding of the educational challenges facing today's students. She also engaged me in conversation that inspired me to think through my ideas and assumptions. I'd also like to thank my sister-in-law, Jo Ann Strowder, for the frequent and inspiring sentiments she expressed throughout this journey. Jo Ann, your words inspired me to sit at the computer long after I was tempted to turn my attention to another project. You've been a tenacious advocate, and I so appreciate the constant reminders that students need direction on how to maximize their college experience to compete in an uncertain job market. A debt of gratitude is also owed to the many parents I encountered at workshops and in other social settings. Thank you for talking candidly to me about your children's struggles in college. Your stories validated my working assumptions and motivated me to make this handbook a reality.

I am grateful to my sister, Dorothy Washington, who invited me to conduct workshops at monthly meetings of the Future Leaders in American Government, an important youth leadership initiative sponsored by Blacks in Government. Those workshops allowed me to test many of my concepts and to get useful feedback from parents and students. A debt of gratitude is also extended to the DC chapter of the Livingstone

James L. Gray, Ed. D.

College National Alumni Association, which also provided opportunities for me to participate in educational workshops and speak at local churches on College Day.

I'm especially grateful to the many students who participated in the focus groups that enriched my understanding of the challenges associated with navigating postsecondary education. And I would be remiss if I didn't thank my daughter, Kristina Gray-Akpa, who's editing of my first draft and helpful hints enabled me to transform a loosely woven manuscript into a respectable handbook with the potential to have a favorable impact on the college experiences of minority and first-generation college students. Lastly, a huge debt of gratitude is owed to Dr. John H. Wulu for the wonderful foreword and the support that he provided throughout my journey to make this book a reality.

Introduction

Education is not received; it is achieved.
—Albert Einstein

Why Write *The College Mentoring Handbook*?

It's easy to assume everyone going to college knows how to manage their learning experience, but they don't. Part of the problem is that no one is giving students appropriate instructions or equipping them with knowledge needed to succeed. My four-fold intent is to

- open their eyes to the new educational realities and demands brought about by the twenty-first century global economy;
- instruct them on how to they can use college to simulate a real-world work experience;
- empower them to maximize their individual uniqueness and develop their human potential; and
- motivate them to think of college in terms of building the requisite skill sets and work readiness capacity to compete in a changing social and economic global landscape.

In the process I want to encourage students to think of themselves as consumers and investors, impressing upon them that earning a degree isn't necessarily a passport to a successful career in an uncertain and ever-changing job market. In fact, I repeatedly make the point that gaining economic independence requires students to build requisite skill sets and competencies that employers seek in prospective college job applicants.

A New Perspective on College Engagement

This publication provides students a comprehensive guidance and unique strategies for managing the college experience and building critical work readiness skill sets in the process. I hope by reading this handbook, young African American and other minority students will embrace the fact that they possess the innate intelligence to become whatever they dream. I'm confident that reading the *Mentoring Handbook* will make them more keenly aware of their intellect and ability to succeed. Likewise, I think reading this book will:

☐ Give students much-needed new perspectives on how to succeed in college despite today's ever-changing educational and economic landscapes.

☐ Help students master the college experience by expanding their capacity and empowering them to take greater personal responsibility for their learning and personal development.

☐ Expand student awareness of the unlimited learning possibilities—and resources—available to them in and around the community campus.

Who's the Audience?

This handbook is written with a broad audience in mind. While students constitute my primary audience, my central aim is to provoke a new conversation about the college experience that draw parents, educators, business leaders, college instructors, administrators, and mentors to the table. I want this cast of characters to understand the new demands and realities of today's postmodern educational landscape, and the greater advocacy placed on them to help maximize student success and the college investment.

I want college instructors and administrators to recognize that in today's postmodern educational environment, the instructor-driven teaching and learning model does not prepare students to compete in the global economy. Students must be encouraged to become self-directed learners and treated accordingly. I want to encourage business leaders to build partnerships with their local colleges and universities and sponsor professionalizing programs and activities to help graduating students build business-related skills and core competences. This handbook will prove to be a vital resource tool to mentors committed to professionalizing student achievement.

Organization of the *Mentoring Handbook*

The *Mentoring Handbook* is organized into eleven mentoring lessons, each containing a discussion and guidance on a critical performance area characteristic of the way of the *self-directed learner*, and which inspires him or her to engineer a rewarding college experience. Students seeking to follow the way of the *self-directed learner* are encouraged to take a notebook and journal their thoughts and insights after reading each mentoring lesson. This is a non-intrusive exercise that will enhance analytical and critical thinking skills. Refer to the table of contents to get a detailed overview of each mentoring lesson. At some point you will want to share this information with like-minded students.

The *Mentoring Handbook* concludes with a summary of mentoring insights and the author's final thoughts on this writing experience. Following the author's final thoughts are several blank pages for students to make notes. Students are invited to treat the *Mentoring Handbook* as a workbook and make notes wherever space permits. Do not be afraid to make marginal notations to share with friends as a teaching tool.

Mentoring Lesson 1

Reframing the College Experience

**The illiterate of the future will not be the
person who does not read. It will be the
person who does not know how to learn.
—Alvin Toffler**

Demystifying the College Degree

It should be clear to readers that an important premise of the
Mentoring Handbook is that a college degree doesn't necessarily
equate with getting a college education. In fact, I'd argue that
students singularly motivated to attain a degree are out of
sync with reality. Let's be clear; getting a degree will not
necessarily prepare a student to participate in a competitive
and uncertain job market. There's more than a subtle
difference in getting a degree and getting an education. In
our fast-paced, postmodern world, it's imperative for students
to focus time and energy on developing work-readiness skill
sets and building employability potential—another central
message illuminated in the *Mentoring Handbook*.

Succeeding in college means planning and designing an
innovative educational experience that produces the requisite
skill sets and core competencies to make students work-
ready. Equally important, succeeding in college must be
about developing employability potential and not just getting
a degree. Leaving college with a degree but without work-
readiness skills isn't good. During a 2011 focus group I
conducted at a small liberal arts college, I discovered that
students were pretty much flying by the seat of their pants. Of
the ten subjects interviewed, only one student had an explicit
plan. The other nine had career ambitions but no plans to
obtain them except making good grades. They confessed that
they just wanted to graduate, and it was clear they thought
a degree guaranteed them a good job in their chosen fields.

During the focus group Q&A, a male student, a junior from a major Midwestern urban city, indicated he had yet to declare a major. He didn't express any concern when probed about competing in a dismal and uncertain job market. Now, in his defense, he was a first-generation student from a family where education was not discussed. Nevertheless, the young man was very articulate, and, except for not having a career goal, he appeared highly intelligent. After further probing, it became clear to me that he was unaware of how to use college as a transitional experience into adulthood and the workforce. Getting a degree in a family with no degrees would become his crowning achievement. I completely understood his motivation and hoped that getting a degree would motivate him to achieve even greater things.

Becoming a Self-Directed Learner

The *Mentoring Handbook* offers students a new way to process and frame the college experience. Essentially, students are instructed on a postmodern college learning model that extends the learning process well beyond the classroom. This model takes into account a vast array of often forgotten growth and learning opportunities in the larger internal and external college community. As a general rule, college for many students is the traditional educational environment characterized by lectures, participatory discussions, group projects, test taking, and grades. From the college curriculum they select a major, and like an empty glass, they go from class to class to get that glass filled with subject-specific information. As a consequence, students limit themselves to an instructor-driven learning experience: following the syllabus, classroom discussions, test taking, and grading. The aim of this book is to get students to think of postsecondary education and personal development as a student-directed learning experience extending beyond the classroom and the boundaries of the college campus.

If I can get students to rethink the outdated traditional instructor-driven college education model that they have fallen victim to, there is a good chance they will take control of their career aspirations. In the process of this paradigm shift, they will become self-directed learners and discover a larger transformational learning community that offers a more rewarding college experience. For example, they would become more acutely aware that:

1. getting a degree doesn't necessarily equate to getting an education;
2. certain academic and career products are more representative of academic success and potential marketplace participation;
3. they can transform college into an exciting, real-world learning experience by becoming self-directed learners;
4. practical learning and development strategies are available, which allow them to gain unique advantages in the job market;
5. college, when used properly, can expose students to real-world work tools and techniques, and enhance work-readiness;
6. imagination and creative thinking become critical tools for shaping career pathways and employability potential; and
7. focusing on cultivating requisite workplace readiness skills and core competences will elevate employability potential.

Good grades are important, as is obtaining a degree. But to compete in a global economy, today's students must focus considerable attention on building skill sets, developing core workplace competences, and gaining the appropriate career-related knowledge. Unfortunately, many college students are woefully ignorant of the world in which they live and are pathetically unaware of the demands this places on their education. They simply are unaware of the real value of college and how to maximize the experience.

Attending college was a major turning point in my life. I had two simple goals when I entered as a first-generation student. My first goal was to get good grades; my second goal was to earn a degree. I figured if I graduated I'd automatically get a job. Although I did graduate from college, I experienced some challenges along the way. A half-century later, I have two master's degrees and a doctorate in education, and I can assure young learners matriculating on college campuses around the country that simply getting good grades and earning a degree aren't enough. It used to be that kids who left home for college were told to make good grades, graduate, and don't bring home any babies. Well, I'm here to say that this long-standing stereotypical approach needs some serious tweaking.

This approach made good sense to me in a robust sixties job market. In fact, many high school graduates skipped college or delayed college altogether because somewhere there were jobs that had their names on them. But that's hardly the case today! Twenty-first-century students face a new technology-driven economy and an uncertain job market that bring into play new educational demands and realities. As a consequence, young men and women going to college need a new set of standards and instructions that speak about student responsibility beyond good grades and getting a degree. To address this new reality, I produced *The College Mentoring Handbook: The Way of the Self-Directed Learner* to inspire a generation of self-directed student to adopt a business-mindset to the college experience.

The Student-Consumer Metaphor

Before tackling the discussion on managing the college experience, I want to take a little time to illuminate the role of the student as *consumer-investor* in the current educational landscape. In the process, we will demystify the college degree as the "ticket" to the job market, particularly in today's economy. My objective is to resituate students' and parents' mind-sets about higher education regarding the notion of educational products. To become better informed on the subject of "students as consumers," an emerging debate among educators and corporate types, I urge students to read the George Cheney article titled "Should We Buy the 'Students-as-Consumer' Metaphor?" You can find it online.

In the meantime, I think we can at least agree that education is an expensive proposition. Likewise, if you're attending college in today's economy, someone is making a great sacrifice. More than ever, it's my position that students and parents must understand that they are indeed consumers and investors in education. Armed with this knowledge, parents need to demand more from the kids they send off to college. They should require them to spend time getting an education as well as earning a degree. In other words, it shouldn't be acceptable to parents for their children to go to college and simply earn degrees without taking full advantage of everything college has to offer them.

Looking at education through the mind-set of a consumer-investor offers parents and students another perspective on the college degree and the endgame of the college experience. Taking into account the cost of college and the uncertainty of the job market, suggest to me that it's time to change the way we think about the college degree. In this new economy, it's imperative that students pay attention to developing work-readiness skills and building employability potential. I believe students can take on this challenge by taking greater personal responsibility for *self-directed learning* and personal development. After all, the postsecondary instructor teaching-learning model, in my estimation, has outlived itself. The *Mentoring Handbook* makes the point that students cannot rely solely on this model to educate and prepare them for jobs in a rapidly emerging society where technology is altering and inventing new jobs every day. It is time for students take on a more aggressive role in the classroom and push instructors to employ and experiment with more innovative real-world teaching and learning strategies, and set learning objectives that reflect global realities.

The Self-Directed Learner as Consumer

In a recent conversation with a first-year student about her performance in college, I was told that a professor almost extinguished her joy of learning with a series of boring lectures. She indicated that despite students' obvious interest in the class, the professor continued with a one-dimensional, instructor-centered teaching method. Feeling short changed she organized a study group, created a learning agenda, and crafted questions that challenged the instructor to elevate the teaching and experience. I shared some of the principles contained in the *Mentoring Handbook* with the young woman, who assured me she would apply them and take responsibility for her education. She subsequently expressed her concerns to the instructor, and, to her surprise, the comments were well received. She was further surprised when the instructor introduced an interactive group learning model that changed the classroom dynamics. This personal story is an example of how a student can create a unique learning and skills building experience by taking personal responsibility. A prospective employer would enjoying hearing this story, and be inclined to hire such person.

In the traditional college classroom, faculty most likely lecture, facilitate classroom discussions, encourage student participation, assign homework and special projects, and give exams. Unfortunately, most students buy into this model. They sit and listen to the lectures and avoid participating in or igniting robust discussions. They confine learning to completing assignments, and just taking exams. In between classes they complain about how boring the classes and instructors are. It never occurs to them that they are equally accountable for their educational success, which means taking ownership for what goes on in the classroom, including collaboration with the instructor. Students must realize that managing the classroom learning, teaching, and teaching experience cultivates personal values that are important behaviors that are transferable to the workplace.

Contrary to what students may think, it is not the job of an instructor to prepare students for jobs. Likewise, the idea that teaching is the sole responsibility of college instructors is a false reality, especially in today's troubled educational landscape. As a "consumer-investor" of education in this postmodern society, students must become more accountable for their education and careers. In fact, accountability is the very foundation of "self-directed learning," an entrepreneurial behavior that prospective employers find appealing in job applicants.

The strategies and tools presented in the *College Handbook* can empower disillusioned students to handle boring and unexciting instructor-centered classroom situations in a very scholarly manner. My experience is that not addressing this situation creates a classroom culture that fosters the attitude of "just get a C and graduate." The resulting problem with this mentality is that low academic performance takes a backseat, and student motivation for learning is retarded. Not to mention that it's especially difficult for a student to cook up success when the focus is solely on degree attainment. Do not short change yourself, work with your classmates to enhance your learning environment and get the quality education that you deserve. This is the essence of personal and professional growth.

Taking Personal Responsibility for Learning

Ultimately, taking responsibility for learning and personal development will empower students to recognize their position in the college learning environment as consumer-investors and change agents. When students actively assume personal responsibility for their learning they gain confidence in engaging faculty in unique and rewarding enriching learning experiences. As suggested in the introduction, self-directed learning is a creative process drawing on and managing the wide range of unique and untapped resources available in college. However, taking personal responsibility is the key.

Beyond the Degree and GPA

A variety of reasons draw students to postsecondary learning institutions across the country. But, ultimately, people attend college to enhance their employment potential in the marketplace and to ensure they're able to function as independent and economically viable citizens. How well they succeed is determined, in large part, by their academic performance. The GPA is an excellent proxy for measuring academic performance, but other factors are also important in predicting college success and indicating one's potential to launch an effective job search. These products convey a more accurate picture of students' work-readiness capacity and employability potential to a prospective employer. They are:

academic portfolio
career/skills portfolio
skills-set profile
resume
curriculum vitae
mentor contacts
career knowledge base
internship history

voluntary service profile
interview journal
biographical statement
social network directory
letters of recommendation
public-speaking profile
conference participation
organizational memberships

Mentoring Lesson 2

Managing the College Experience

It is not that we have so little time but that we lose so much. ... The life we receive is not short but we make it so; we are not ill provided but use what we have wastefully.
—Seneca, *On the Shortness of Life*

The Student Manager

I contend that the biggest challenge facing students today is how to manage the four years spent in college, and, second, how to properly engage in the learning experience. From time to time, students have told me that college was boring, and they were not having any fun in college. In fact, several students who returned to college after dropping out said they left because college was boring. But the more I probed them, the real problem was one of time management. They always appeared shocked when told that the purpose of going to college isn't to have fun, and it has never been. And given how rapidly the global economy is changing, and the cost of college, students need to put fun on hold.

To heighten student awareness and understanding of this challenge, I have identified seven prominent management-engagement areas. How students handle these management-engagement areas directly impacts their academic performance and professional development and the extent to which they lay the groundwork for their career paths.

1. Time
2. Learning
3. Course work
4. Faculty relationships
5. Career pathway
6. Peer relationships
7. Work readiness opportunities

The seven management-engagement areas are all interconnected. In fact, time is a key aspect in each area, which accounts for the lengthy discussion on time management. Accordingly, the seven management-engagement areas receive less than full treatments in this section. However, students will find comments on these areas in other parts of the *Mentoring Handbook*. For example, in the robust presentation in "Mentoring Lesson 1: Reframing the College Experience," managing learning and course work are prominently mentioned. For now, let's focus attention on time management.

Time Is on Your Side

For all practical purposes, students have sufficient time to invent a career and build quality skill sets to compete successfully in the global marketplace. But far too many students see college as a social experiment in newly found independence. As a result, they get hooked on having fun. And if their goal is to just do enough to get a degree and graduate, then their use of time becomes misguided. In the end, this attitude will retard a student's best of intentions for getting an education. The result is a marginally prepared job seeker with marginal job opportunities.

The chart below (Time Management Table) gives students and parents a sense of the time available to students over a four-year (1,460 days) period to get the job done. From a time management perspective, wisely using the "*table,*" students have more than enough time to enhance their employability potential and transform themselves into highly qualified job seekers. Some students might take five years; others will graduate in three and half years, but the point is whatever they do with their time, their time will do to them.

The College Time Management Converter Table		
One Day	24 Hours	-------
One Week	168 Hours	-------
One Month	720 Hours	-------
One Year	8,760 Hours	365 Days
Four Years	35,040 Hours	1,460 Days

I come in contact with a number of educators by virtue of my wife having been a former high school teacher in two systems; and I have learned that in addition to poor writing skills, students generally lack time management In fact, the general sentiment among educators and business people I talk with is that the vast majority of young men and women entering college today lack basic time management skills. This is a more compelling issue especially for first-generation college students. If kids don't develop strong time management skills while attending college, they will be woefully unprepared to compete with their generation of job seekers. It is quite likely that they will not take full advantage of the learning opportunities available to them. The worst case scenario is, by mismanaging time, a student is likely to become overwhelmed by competing academics and a misguided social agenda. Coupled with the absence of an explicit plan for succeeding in college is one reason why students become college dropouts.

Managing the Learning Process

Taking responsibility for learning means exhibiting leadership and accountability, which require students to set explicit learning goals and career objectives in a personalized plan, the centerpiece of the *Mentoring Handbook*. As pointed out in "Mentoring Lesson 1: Reframing the College Experience," the student has to take active responsibility for his/her personal learning! *Self-directed learners* understand the accountability dynamic and take full advantage of the endless reservoir of transformational learning and growth opportunities on and beyond the walls of the campus. Sadly, with no parents nearby to monitor their behavior, coupled with newfound freedoms, students are reluctant to develop a plan. They might have an idea in their heads nut nothing written down on paper.

When engaging college students in a discussion on the subject of taking personal responsibility for their own learning, I strongly urge them to develop a plan. I also convey to them ways in which to approach to manage the learning process:

11

- Look for ways to explore learning as a creative process.
- Develop endgame skill sets and career-related technical knowledge.
- Identify and engage in internal and external learning opportunities.
- Routinely assess their learning strengths and weaknesses.
- Seek feedback from faculty and mentors.
- Take a leadership role in the classroom.
- Help other students to attain personal learning goals.

Managing Course Work

Managing course work is a key engagement area in the overarching learning management system. The inability to manage course load effectively leads to major disruptions in a student's academic life. An often overlooked management tool is the syllabus that each student is routinely given on the first day of class. In effect, it is the instructor's plan, telling students about the course load. The assignments are spelled out in detail and have clearly specified product delivery dates. Taking the syllabi from all of your classes, you in effect have a significant part of an individual development plan. This topic is covered in greater detail in *Mentoring Lesson 3: Blueprinting a Path to Success.*

Managing Faculty Relationships

The *Mentoring Handbook* places high importance on faculty-student relationships. Based on my conversation with students, managing faculty relationships is something students rarely consider as part of personal and professional growth opportunities. Other than the classroom, students are reluctant to pursue purposeful interactions with faculty. It is disappointing that students don't see the value faculty relationships beyond the classroom. Writing this handbook is my opportunity to stress the importance of establishing relationships with faculty and including them in social networks. A self-directed learner takes full view of faculty as powerful resource agents. The passive student, who is looking to be fed, on the hand, fails to see the larger role faculty play as essential actors in the learning environment.

The discussion on the importance of faculty relationships is continued in *Mentoring Lesson 6: Collaborative Learning* in greater detail.

Managing Your Career Path

Managing the career path is about making good choices regarding one's professional future. Having a personalized development plan is an indication that a student has a sense of professional direction and is exploiting every opportunity to avail himself or herself of the resources in the learning environment. Meeting and connecting with individuals in the certain career field to keep up with industry trends is an important aspect of managing one's career path. I would also encourage students to check out online career toolkits; this is always a useful career path management and planning strategy.

In explaining my thoughts in a recent discussion with a friend about the concept of college as a management experience, I was encouraged to include a discussion of the importance of focusing attention on managing one's career path. I was reminded that in today's world of work, it is virtually impossible to stay on the job and retire years later in the same job. So the message is that career paths have starting points, but they are rarely a straight line in today's society. By establishing faculty relationships, students create access to resource agents who can help them navigate their career paths.

Managing Peer Relationships

Even the most well-intended and most motivated student can go astray academically because of the inability to regulate competing social priorities, especially peer relationships. As a consequence, they misuse precious time just chilling. Students who mismanage peer relationships will usually to graduate and leave college with a degree, but they leave with a marginal education and questionable work readiness skill sets.

Making friends and building peer relationships are salient characteristics impacting college success. However, students must guard against letting peer interactions marginalize academic performance. In the end, managing peer relationships is about monitoring the time and opportunities set aside for peer socialization. I refer students back to the SWRP as a tool to monitor the seven "management engagement areas."

Students come to college under a great deal of pressure to excel in their academics, and then they struggle to not give in to peer pressures. But I'm confident that by adopting the *self-directed learner* approach to college, students can find the strength to resist moments of homesickness and other harmful and marginalizing behaviors. In effect, the goals and objectives and timelines specified in the SWRP provide the guidance students need in determining how to allocate time for academics and their social life

Managing Work Readiness Opportunities

On a practical level, a work readiness opportunity is no more than the engagement in a set of on or off campus learning situations where students can acquire selected technical knowledge, and build workplace skills and core competences. Managing these learning and personal growth circumstances is an act of personal accountability, a major characteristic of the self-directed learner. At the core of the managing work readiness opportunities is making the best use of your educational tools, time, and learning circumstances to enhance your employability potential. The work readiness concept is a central theme highlighted throughout the *Mentoring Handbook*.

Time Management Tools

I hope reading the *Mentoring Handbook* will cause students to stop and think for a moment, and realize that the skills, tools, and techniques they use to time manage the college experience are the same ones used by people in a variety of organizations and career disciplines. Hence, it is important for students to reframe the college experience and use the time to build skill sets that are transferable to the real world of work instead of wasting time. Be assured that the day will come when an interviewer or prospective employer calls a former instructor or another reference and is told that "aside from occasionally missing deadlines, John/Mary was a good worker." Or that he/she "was a good student but was usually late turning in assignments."

Students, how you manage your time will make impressions on those around you. What you do with your time while in college will be reflected in transcript, resume, your portfolio, and the way you are able to handle an interview. We don't usually get second chances to make a first impression, so I implore you to make a serious effort to manage your time well. Get in a habit of using activity logs, day-monthly planners, calendars, and to-do lists, all of which are very practical and effective time management tools. Include them in your portfolio as evidence of your time-management acumen.

Applying these tools during the development and execution of a student plan will get you comfortable with the planning process, another very fundamental workplace skill set. Make it a point to share your college time-management successes with prospective employers during interviews. They will likely find you more appealing than other candidates seeking the same job. Describe the tools and techniques successfully used to manage a challenging course schedule, extracurricular activities, study sessions and peer learning groups, and competing assignments and special projects. A special project could be a situation where students planned, designed a learning group, or facilitated a career seminar.

Take a few minutes when time permits and go online and check out some of the more sophisticated project management tools—for example, the Gantt Milestone Chart and the PERT Chart, which are the more traditional time and project management tools. There is a premium on hiring individuals in today's evolving global work culture who can manage projects. In a recent conversation with my daughter and another young lady, both of whom are project managers with salaries approaching six figures, I was told to stress the importance of project management skills in today's workplace. What made them highly effective project managers was using the college experience to acquire the basic skill sets described in *"Mentoring Lesson 4: Building Employability Potential."*

Mentoring Lesson 3

Blueprinting the Path to Success

**Always plan ahead. It wasn't raining when Noah
built the ark.
—Richard Cushing**

Your Educational Journey Requires a Plan

It should clear to you now that college is serious business. And like any business, a good plan is required to ensure success. A plan gives students a basic tool to manage the college experience. A personalized plan enables students to make better use of the college experience as a training ground for building real-world skill sets and growing employability potential. I am proposing that students develop a Student Work Readiness Plan (SWRP). Preparing and implementing a SWRP puts a student in the role of a self-directed leaner.

Ideally, students should enter college with a well-developed idea of how they plan to use the college experience. Considering the high cost of college today, you'd think parents would insist that their sons and daughters sit down and devise a plan of action before departing for college. To the contrary, many students, especially those who are the first in their families to attend college, arrive on campus unsure of what they want to get from the college experience. To compound the dilemma, these kids like so many students have no idea how to navigate the daunting college experience, let alone plan a career.

Simply put, the SWRP is a set of actions describing how a student uses the college learning experience, to build personal work readiness capacity and enhance employability potential. The plan is composed of a set of written statements (goals) describing what a student intends to accomplish with the resources available to him/her inside and outside the classroom. It reflects how a student will go about the business of managing their course work: using their time, seeking learning growth opportunities, using campus resources, engaging faculty, and building requisite workplace skill sets.

Benefits from having of a SWRP are as follows:

☐ It is an excellent indicator of a student's commitment to academic pursuits and personal growth.
☐ It also communicates how a student will go about the business of managing and best experiencing a life-changing event that is best experienced when guided by a well-thought-out plan of action. .
☐ It is an excellent tool for engaging mentors and career coaches, interacting with faculty, and collaborating with fellow students around common career aspirations.
☐ Ultimately, a plan signifies a student's acceptance that he or she has the responsibility for his or her education and personal development.
☐ It empowers students to cultivate and apply a business mind-set to the college learning experience that is transferable to the real world of work.

Without an explicit plan of action, students will likely leave college with fewer documentable skill sets and growth experiences from which to build an attention-getting resume demonstrating quality workplace readiness skills.

The Student Employment Development Plan

The SWRP development is a process. Not only is it easy, it is a highly transformative learning experience that builds an array of real-world transferable skills and competences: time management, communication and writing skills, public speaking, teamwork, conflict management resolution, giving and receiving feedback, teamwork, project management, leadership, organization and planning, goals setting, and activity evaluation. Start the SWRP development process by reviewing and defining in explicit terms your purpose for attending college and your career aspiration.

Pondering the nine questions below is a simple exercise that will help get you started.

1. Is your principle interest to acquire a strong background in a particular field?
2. Is it to get the knowledge necessary to become a contributing member of society?
3. Are you looking to make connections and build strong student-faculty relationships?
4. Are you trying to increase your earning power?
5. Are you in college to ensure you increase your chances of having ample job opportunities?
6. Or are you in college simply to become a well-rounded person?
7. Are you being productive until you find yourself?
8. Are you delaying having to get a job?
9. Is your intention to build employability potential?

The circumstances motivating an individual to attend college ultimately impact the development, quality, and overall direction of the SWRP. It is useful for students to also have personal visions—that is, a sense of what they ultimately want to accomplish as a result of obtaining a college education. This is, in essence, an inspirational statement of the future a student intends to create, and the motivation for building his/her career pathway.

Once a student is clear and confident in what his/her purpose and career focus are, the next step is to decide on a major. I advocate doing this by the close of the freshman year, if not sooner. Time wasted is a lost opportunity for purposeful learning, skills building, and enhancing employability potential. Students who have yet to settle on an area of study are advised to take a few minutes and ponder the questions below to get a sense of what career pathway might be most suitable for them.

- What things are you most passionate about?
- What type of jobs most interest you?
- What are your special skills?
- What contribution do you want to make to society?
- What career would allow you to live in a safe community?
- What type of work would you most enjoy doing?
- What were your favorite subjects in school?

- ☐ What unique and interesting hobbies do you have?
- ☐ What previous work experience did you enjoy?
- ☐ What jobs or professional people do you find interesting?

You can do this exercise with other students, whether they have declared a major or not. Take a sheet of paper and scribble your responses. Then refer to the course-offering guide and select two or three majors that might interest you. Talk to friends with similar interest in these majors and the instructors teaching the courses to gather their impressions. Go online and gather information about career potentials, the job favorability, industry trends, and skill requirements.

Deciding on a Career

When deciding on a career, take the time to investigate the job opportunities in your career field and how they match up with your career aspirations. Also, when it comes to your career focus, make sure that your major aligns with your career interests. Students should have some idea of the doors your course work will open for you. It is suggested that you talk with a mentor or a faculty to get advice. You can visit the campus counseling or career service center for advice. In the final analysis, however, it is important that you know where your interests lie and the things that motivate you, and the things and people that you enjoy working with.

Arriving on campus without a game plan or clear academic focus is a potential train wreck waiting to happen. But it is a reality in today's world. So if you have yet to "declare" insofar as a major is concerned, chill out but don't delay the process any longer than necessary. Starting classes without any clue of your intended field of study can be costly. Too many incoming freshmen find themselves in this situation, often uncertain of a major after they've been in school for two or more semesters.

In a recent seminar with a cohort of men discussing factors impacting academic performance and job preparation, a young man who was in his junior year had yet to declare a major. When asked what he intended to do after graduation, he simply said that he had a C average and planned to graduate on time. He was fairly confident he could find a "decent job" upon graduation. After the focus group ended, I suggested that he visit an adviser to review his transcript and determine what career pathway would be most appropriate for him, given his situation.

Setting Goals for the Journey

Defining your purpose and identifying a field of interest will help you formulate a realistic set of academic and career goals—that is, sequenced and time-phased statements about what you want to achieve and by when. For example, not later than a month after graduation, you want to have accepted a job offer. Goal statements imply that a set of specific activities must be performed in order to achieve your goal. Continuing with the aforementioned example, you would have prepared an attention getting resume, participated in several practice interviews, built a power network, attended several job fairs, and performed in several internships. In effect, goals provide the framework for organizing the actions one takes to attain the goal and to write a plan.

A well-thought-out goal statement reflects a student's academic and career pathway and communicates what is to be accomplished during a specific time frame. You are more likely to accomplish a goal that is written down on paper. Putting goals in clear and concise written statements that you can periodically review enhances your chances for accomplishing them.

- Limit a goal statement to a single, concise, and compelling sentence.
- Align your goals with your statement of purpose, personal vision, and career aspirations.
- Students are urged to confer with their parents, faculty, and mentors when formulating goals to ensure that they are aligned and set a realistic course of action.

Your goals will convey what you plan to do to achieve your purpose for attending college. For all practical terms, a goal is a specific performance target. Students can reference the Internet to get an idea for goals they should have in college. Below is suggested language you may want to consider when formulating SWRP goals:

- ☐ Complete internships during my junior and senior years.
- ☐ Join two campus-based student organizations to strengthen my leadership capacity.
- ☐ Join at least two professional organizations by the end of my junior year to grow my social network.
- ☐ Build and activate a career-oriented social network to support a job search.
- ☐ Collaborate on a unique student-faculty learning or research project to grow my resume and people skills.
- ☐ Organize a peer learning group to support academic performance and career development options.
- ☐ Participate in a travel-abroad experience by the end of my junior year.
- ☐ Use college to simulate a real-world work experience.

By actively engaging in the goal-setting process in college, students cultivate a major work-readiness skill that's commonplace in all companies and organizations. College goal-setting and prioritization are documentable skill sets that can be included on the resume. This is just another example of how students can creatively use the college experience to enhance their competitiveness in the job market and build transferable skill sets.

Exercise. Take a sheet of paper and answer the nine questions below. They are posed to stimulate additional thinking about populating the SWRP, and to help students think about and formulate concise and compelling academic and career-related goal statements.

1. How do I engage faculty outside of the classroom?
2. How do I manage to know what I really want to do with my life?
3. How do I make college my highest priority?
4. What are my talents and strengths?
5. What weaknesses must I improve to better prepare myself?

6. What specific academic/technical knowledge do I need to acquire?
7. How do I better organize and manage learning opportunities?
8. What skill sets will enhance my employability potential?
9. Are my goals measureable and realistic?

Carefully analyze your written responses and specify actions you might take to achieve your goals. I suggest students start with at least three goal statements and eventually add one or two more goals as they progress toward graduation.

Write your goals at the top of a single page and list ways to achieve the goals underneath. For example, a goal to "organize and initiate a job search by the start of the second semester of the junior year" might combine the following related activities: prepare and fashion an appropriate resume and cover letter, update and finalize an attention-getting biographical statement, schedule several career-related practice interviews, and seek support from faculty and mentors to identify several informal interviews. Refer to Lesson 9 *(Interviewing with Confidence)* for more discussion on the informal interview.

Each semester, review your goals and the tasks and activities you intend to pursue to achieve them, and take the opportunity to correct any shortfalls. Performing this progress appraisal activity could likely result in revising career options and discovering new resources and learning opportunities.

Writing an effective SWRP requires students to familiarize themselves with academic and career-related educational products, which will be a new concept to many. In my opinion, academic and career-related educational products represent a new conversation about the college endgame and the very essence of the learning process. This is a major feature in the SWRP development process, suggesting a product-driven outcome as opposed to the more "traditional degree-driven" approach. In the latter approach, students are less likely to focus attention on acquiring work readiness skills sets and building employability potential. In effect, the concept of academic and career-related products lays a foundation for reframing the college experience and student educational expectations. Refer to the Sample SWRP Format on the next page to get an idea of how you might proceed in preparing your personalized plan.

Student Employment Development Plan Benefits

The SWRP development process introduces students to skills that are transferable to the real-world workplace: writing, planning, organization, management, goal setting, project management, and leadership skills. Companies are desperate to find college graduates with these skill sets. Developing a SWRP also exposes students to the concept of work breakdown analysis, time-phasing and sequencing work products, performance monitoring, and evaluation. Students electing not to develop a SWRP will miss out on an awesome learning experience.

Suggested SWRP Format

Fall Semester /__/ Spring Semester /__/ Summer Vacation /__/

Mentor _____Date_____

What is your purpose for attending college?

In not more than three short sentences, describe your personal mission.

What is your career focus?

What goals do you want to accomplish in the fall and spring semesters, and the summer in each calendar year?

What actions will you take to accomplish each goal?

Activities. (What's necessary in order to accomplish your objectives?)

What specific skills do you need to develop or improve?

What specific academic/career products do you intend to target?

_____   _____

Mentor's Signature   **Date**

_____   _____

Career Counselor's Signature   **Date**

This is just a suggested SWRP plan using a question format to help students develop their plans. It is okay to ask around or visit the Internet to find other formats with which you are comfortable. The central idea is that it is important to adopt and commit to a plan to ensure that you develop your human potential and maximize the learning experience in which you and your family have invested. I would encourage you to share your plan with your mentor and career counselor. Their sign-off on the plan will signify their concurrence and support in assisting you throughout the SWRP.

Evaluating Personal Progress

Get in the habit of routinely evaluating the progress made on your SWRP. Do this for two fundamental reasons. First, you should want to know how well you're doing. After all, there is a huge investment of money and your personal time and energy involved in your educational journey. I would hope your expectation is to succeed. Second, you should want to develop the capacity and know-how to conduct evaluations. As mentioned on multiple occasions, the SWRP development process and strategies expose students to skill sets and core competencies that are transferable to the real-world workplace.

The goals and corresponding subtasks and activities set forth in the SWRP form the basis for student evaluations. To get you started, I have outlined six questions below. You may also pull together a cohort of classmates to perform a group evaluation, an experience that can be used to build and showcase your planning and organization acumen.

1. Look at the actionable items and the respective timelines and simply ask whether you did what you said you would in the allotted time.
2. Determine what you were able to accomplish and why.
3. Look at actions that weren't achieved and why.
4. Review your goal statements and subtasks to make certain they were realistic and measurable.
5. Taking the timelines into account, decide if you took on too much or just didn't commit to getting the job done.
6. Carefully and objectively analyze your findings and decide what has to be done to get back on track so you can execute your SWRP.

Written responses to the six questions will produce the best assessment of your progress. The writing process will encourage more thoughtful consideration of overall educational performance and progress, including your values and work ethics. It's recommended that students evaluate their progress at the end of each semester. It's advisable that students should share their progress and concerns with their mentors and faculty supporters. Sharing your evaluation findings and analyses will generate constructive feedback that can enhance academic performance and progress.

Mentoring Lesson 4

Building Employability Potential

Our work is the presentation of our capabilities.
—Unknown

Building Work Readiness Skill Sets

Today's job seekers are faced with a pretty dismal job market, mounting economic uncertainty, and global competition. The *Mentoring Handbook* shares with students the skill sets employers seek. While it's certainly true that companies seek individuals with the technical capacity to impact organizational missions and goals, my experience has been that they find job applicants with a broad mix of employability skills more attractive. Students have the opportunity to use the college experience to strengthen existing skills and develop new ones. I suggest students use their four years in college to get comfortable with the employability skills and qualities listed below, what I also refer to as work-readiness skills:

self-motivation	public speaking
critical thinking	planning
active listening	organizing
analysis	coordinating
verbal communication	facilitating
written communication	project management
people skills	adaptability
risk-taker	leadership

From the beginning of freshman year to the time you graduate, focus attention on cultivating and mastering these skills and core competences. By doing so, you will gain a distinct advantage over other applicants in the job pools where you compete. I classify these transferable skills into four broad categories: basic workplace skills and executive functioning skills. I also provide students brief remarks on what are considered executive and soft skills, digital skills, and global skills.

Executive Functioning Skills

An overriding sentiment expressed to me by several teachers and business leaders is that high school and college students often lack executive functioning skills. That is the ability to plan, organize, manage, analyze, coordinate, and facilitate. It has always been my position that executive skills are critical to achieving mission-driven goals and priorities. That's why I always advise students to make it a priority to sharpen their executive functioning skill sets. Make it a goal in your SWRP. Having a handle on executive skills and possessing strong oral and written communication skills, and being able think critically, gives students a unique advantage over other job applicants.

Soft Skills

In today's market, soft skills are equally important to employers. In fact, companies devote considerable resources on "soft skills" training because business etiquette, employee friendliness, and other personal qualities impact productivity and profits. Companies will take a good look at applicants demonstrating capacity to work professionally and pleasantly with the public. I have been involved in a number of interviews over the course of a nearly forty-year career, and I can tell you that job applicants with the requisite technical skills and high GPAs don't always get the job.

I urge students to review the list of "soft skills" below and identify those areas needing improvement. The college learning environment is a perfect place to practice soft skills and other mixed employability skills. Also, visit the Internet to expand your knowledge and appreciation of soft skills in today's workplace. The soft skills are:

positive personality	active listening
confidence	sense of humor
effective communication	good telephone etiquette

trustworthiness
team player
pleasant attitude
adaptable to change
self-motivated
assertiveness
ability to negotiate
thoughtfulness
interpersonal
honesty and integrity

professional attitude
strong work ethic
personal accountability
company loyalty
passion for one's work
openness to learn
entrepreneurial attitude
punctuality
risk-taker

Global Workplace Skill Sets

For the past several years, I have been engaged in public-private health and business projects in Africa. My travel has afforded me the opportunity to meet people in the highest seats of government and business. What has become very apparent to me is that the emerging global economy places new realities and demands on students pursuing a college education in the twenty-first century. You are part of a borderless world economy, and as a consequence you will find yourself competing with the best and brightest from around the globe. Master the list of skills provided below and sharpen your global skills capacity.

- ☐ Sensitivity to a "borderless" global community
- ☐ Worldview critical thinking
- ☐ Global cultural awareness
- ☐ Global ecological awareness
- ☐ Knowledge of global social and economic issues
- ☐ Awareness of global governance issues
- ☐ Strong knowledge of world geography
- ☐ Heightened awareness of diverse world perspectives
- ☐ Understanding of global decision-making strategies
- ☐ Knowledge of marketplace lexicon
- ☐ Analytical reasoning and creativity

The self-directed learner will master the list and make an effort to become an active participant in the global community. He/she can do this by traveling abroad at some point during his/her college career. Traveling abroad will profoundly impact your educational preparedness and diversity. Also, he/she will make it a habit to become familiar with global issues: read books and newspapers, watch cable news from around the world, take global-focused courses, become pen pals to students in a foreign country, and establish discussion groups with students from other parts of the global to explore social and economic issues.

Digital Technology Skills

I have five family members who have worked in the higher echelons of digital technology environments. And I have repeatedly heard from them that students must focus on building digital literacy in today's global economy. This means acquiring strong skill sets in the use of technology and communication tools: data and information management, knowledge management, and computer hardware and software applications. In light of the heavy dependence on digital technology in business around the globe, no matter one's major field of study, workers across every discipline are required to be digitally literate. Subsequently, pursuing a minor field of study in computer systems and information technology is highly recommended as a way to enhance one's work-readiness potential.

Personal and Workplace Values

Part of my responsibility as a manger was to make sure that the right employee was hired. Ideally, that individual had to contribute to the success of the organization. In addition to assessing the skill sets and core competences of the list of suitable candidates provided from the personnel office, I would take into account personal values. Why? Because values set the tone for an organization's culture, and I learned over the years that culture impacts climate. Needless to say, when I was often confronted with a candidate for a vacancy who had great skills but questionable personal values, that individual was not considered.

This is more the case today than at any time in the workplace. Today managers consider personal values as critical attributes of a "good" employee, the basis for providing quality customer service. Your values show in academic performance, how you manage relationships with faculty and peers, and other behavior. How you make decisions and set priorities are other aspects of the college experience that employers will look at. The purpose of asking questions about your mission and purpose in life, during an interview, is to get insights into your personal value system.

To help students get a handle on the personal values they possess and what they might need to work on, I designed a self-appraisal exercise. Have fun with this exercise by making it a game you can play with your peer group. Add pizza and soda, and you have a party!

Personal Values Appraisal Profile

The personal values listed below are a few examples of what organizations find attractive in their employees. The list came out of a discussion with a group of friends who were interested in knowing where I was in finishing the *Mentoring Handbook*. This input represents their contribution. On that particular evening we generated a personal values profile to help with comfortable talking about personal values.

Student Personal Values Appraisal Profile

accountability	passion giving
commitment	respect
consistency	teamwork
diversity	risk-taker
efficiency	service
stewardship	responsibility
empathy	accuracy
courage	respect
empowerment	dedication
humor	enjoyment/fun
innovation	wisdom
integrity	independence
courage	influence
ownership	learning

compassion	loyalty
friendliness	credibility
discipline	honesty
order	innovativeness
fair play	excellence
dependability	empowerment
flexibility	dignity

Create a personal values profile by ranking each item using a scale from 1 to 10. No, the exercise isn't scientifically based, but it will give you a good idea of what you need to improve, provided you're honest in performing the self-appraisal. In this exercise, 10 represents an "exceptional" ranking; 5 signifies an "average" ranking, and 1 signifies a "deficit" ranking. Numbers falling within the five-point interval are interpreted accordingly. For example, a rank of 7 is "slightly above" average; while a ranking of 3 is considered a poor ranking. Remember, the sole purpose of this exercise is to give students an idea of the improvements they have to make.

Documenting Employability Potential

Former work associates who have yet to retire from public and private sector organizations have shared with me that portfolios are once again gaining popularity among prospective employers. Because they're good sources of information from which to evaluate a job applicant, more employers are requesting them in interviews. Having a portfolio in today's economic climate just makes good sense! It's an important tool used to organize and manage educational products developed during college and displays one's achievements, skill sets, and abilities.

Well-constructed portfolios are invaluable personal marketing tools and are excellent for interview preparation. In fact, portfolios can often be the key to getting a job! Students looking for an advantage in a dismal job market should develop portfolios. A carefully crafted portfolio will afford a prospective employer unique insights into a student's academic performance, personal values system, campus and community leadership, classroom achievements, executive functioning skills, propensity to work in teams, adaptability to change, relationship-building attributes, and communication capacity. My experience has been that portfolios actually present a much larger picture of a job applicant than do resumes and reference letters.

Students are encouraged to take their portfolios to every interview. You may not be asked to present it, but if the question arises, you'll have it. And, trust me, employers will be impressed even if they don't ask to peruse them. Also, portfolios

☐ serve as essential tools for enhancing career-development capacity;
☐ demonstrate evidence of skill sets, subject-matter knowledge, and enterprise;
☐ provide a frame of reference for personal evaluation and self-discovery; and
☐ provide a creative approach for tracking and recording career-related and real-world learning experiences and evidence of work readiness.

Organizing a College Portfolio

In reality, the portfolio is just a file cabinet where you keep documentation of accomplishments and professional growth. Your portfolio conveys your employability potential. From that information, students can produce resumes, curricula vitas, biographical statements, and other important documents relevant to job searches. What goes into the portfolio is determined by the success a student has achieving academic and career goals outlined in the SWRP. To construct an academic-career portfolio, simply devise a system of folders for each portfolio element listed below.

Elements of the Academic-Career Portfolio

work history	core competences
community service	certificates
volunteer service	awards/special honors
skill sets	professional memberships

conferences/workshops	resume/CV
public speaking	mentor file
campus affiliations	history of internships
publications	interview journal
special projects	biostatement
career-goal statement	support letters
transcript	affiliations
travel abroad	network directory

My nephew, who is an educator, recently shared with me just prior to sending this manuscript to the publishers that he presented his portfolio in an interview for a teaching position. He was certain that the portfolio was a critical factor in getting several job offers. Traditionally, teachers have been using the job portfolio for years, but there is no reason for job seekers in other career fields not to use it to showcase their unique accomplishments, experience, and skill sets. You can begin developing your portfolio in your freshman year; by the time you graduate, you will have assembled a large volume of professional development materials. Based on a particular job interview or organization, you will customize your portfolio as appropriate. The interview portfolio is an excellent tool to use in getting a job, so make sure that it is part of your job search campaign.

Mentoring Lesson 5

Collaborative Learning

A small group of thoughtful people could change the world. Indeed, it's the only thing that ever has.
—Margaret Mead

Learning Is Not a Spectator Sport

As a manager of a national federal grant initiative, I used collaborative learning techniques as a strategy to help my staff to improve overall program performance and operation effectiveness. Collaborative learning is a practical way for students to enhance academic performance and professional development and build indispensable teamwork skills. There are any number ways students can form collaborative learning groups; they will generally find whatever form agreed upon to be manageable and reasonably productive.

My experience has been that the level of group engagement and productivity is limited only by one's imagination and the commitment of the participants. I found collaborative learning in the form of peer learning to be especially effective when I wrote my dissertation. The group was comprised of a handpicked cohort of seven candidates pursuing the doctorate degree in education. Ideally, the group engaged in interactive discussions and work activities driven by planned agendas addressing research issues of individual and collective interest. The mutual support and individual commitment to the process enabled all seven participants to complete their dissertations and graduate together.

Why Form Learning Groups?

Forming learning groups is a great way to maximize the college experience through mutual learning agendas. Like-minded classmates can employ this concept to build confidence, organize collaborative learning projects, and explore a variety of learning opportunities. By participating in learning groups, students begin to realize they're limited only by their own imaginations.

Don't allow the artificial walls separating the community and the classroom retard your chances for real-world learning opportunities. Forming a learning group is an excellent way to liberate yourself from your college campus and explore the surrounding community. If you are a freshman beginning your second semester, make an effort to form peer-learning groups. In each year thereafter, experience participating in and organizing peer-learning groups. To foster group cohesiveness and to make the learning groups manageable, it's recommended that each group not exceed five students. Likewise, those students should share a common academic and/or career focus, and ground rules should be set at the outset of the first meeting. By the way, it is one thing to join a peer-learning group, but it's another thing to organize one. And you'd better believe being the organizer of a peer-learning group is an attention-grabber on a resume.

The Transformative Power of Learning Groups

Through peer learning groups, students create additional support systems to promote educational enrichment and professional growth. By working in small groups, students have more opportunities to

☐ strengthen their public speaking skills;
☐ build confidence in working in teams;
☐ discuss issues and questions germane to their career fields;
☐ share information and resources about jobs;
☐ design activities that promote intellectual stimulation and critical thinking; and
☐ provide space to clarify classroom discussions and complex concepts.

Equally beneficial, group participation creates additional opportunities for students to assume meaningful leadership roles and acquire managing skills and techniques, negotiating group strategies, and resolving disagreements. Moreover, the group experience improves communication skills, heightens self-esteem, fosters social and interpersonal skills, and can enhance interview skills. These benefits will give a student a unique advantage in the applicant pool when seeking employment.

Suggestions for Forming a Learning Group

As suggested above, learning groups are most productive when peers share a common purpose, are goal-oriented, and demonstrate a keen sense of commitment to purpose. During friendly conversations with classmates, inquire about their academic expectations. Ask if they want to form study groups to share thoughts on their career goals and other themes of interest to them. You want to avoid inviting peers to your study group who

- are likely to indulge in excessive social activity;
- show questionable interest in academics;
- make it a practice to cram overnight for exams;
- practice dishonest tactics to get good grades;
- show a tendency to manipulate classmates;
- get others to writer their papers.

Find people who have the same goals and aspirations as you do; avoid classmates who demonstrate misguided social and academic agendas. Likewise, don't work with individuals who are okay with being mediocre or unfocused academic performers. They will be a negative influence on the learning group. It doesn't always happen, but when you hang around people who aren't really going anywhere, before too long you're moving in the same direction. When I was growing up, my grandmother was always checking out my friends, and on occasions she would say, "Son, watch the company you keep, because if you lie with sleeping dogs you're bound to get fleas."

Faculty Engagement Matters

The *Mentoring Handbook* places high importance on faculty-student relationships. Make no mistake about it, relationship building is a critical ingredient for cooking up college success. This holds true for the college learning environment as well as professional places of work. Purposeful interactions between students and faculty contribute to a quality college experience. Whenever I have an opportunity to talk with college kids or to conduct workshops for them, it truly disappoints me to hear students say they usually don't talk to faculty outside of the classroom. When I hear that, my response is to remind them that engaging in meaningful conversations with instructors, wherever you find them on campus, is a right that comes with the tuition you pay. You are paying for this privilege, so take full advantage of faculty as resource agents. It shows poor judgment not to make good use of them, especially since faculty members are essential actors in the learning environment.

Faculty fully understand that students have to function in the emerging global society. They know the challenges shaping students' careers, and they can give solid advice on what classes you should be taking to achieve your goals. Besides offering academic help or advice, faculty members also write reference letters for students who are trying to get in grad school or obtain their first job. And don't forget that faculty members have friends and relatives who are leaders at major companies and organizations that are always looking to hire college graduates. Take my advice and make it a priority to work with faculty and staff. Although staffers don't teach, many have also achieved academic success and are as credentialed as faculty. They also are engaged in power social networks. So networking with staff makes good sense and is a source for building effective student social networks!

Benefits from Faculty Engagement

Remember, it's your education, and what you do with it is limited only by your imagination. Practice being bold and creative, and don't hesitate to carry that sense of empowerment with you on job or to graduate school interviews. Take advantage of the strategies and suggestions provided in *The* Mentoring *Handbook* and begin to build strong interactive relationships with several faculty members. If you do that, I guarantee you'll enjoy a productive college experience. As indicated, below are several significant benefits derived from faculty engagement.

interpersonal skills	interview opportunities
professionalism	letters of recommendation
support graduate studies	job search guidance
facilitate ideas	career plans
support student interests	share industry trends
assist with publications	leadership activities
job opportunities	facilitate internships
builds social networks	advocates/mentors

It bears repeating that students are consumer-investors engaged in a costly education and learning experience, and drawing on faculty knowledge is a priority of the highest magnitude. Missing the opportunity to collaborate with faculty diminishes the potential for academic excellence and professional growth. Before going into Mentoring Lesson 6, take a minute to peruse the benefits derived from faculty-student relationships. Take a sheet of paper and make a short list of a few things you can do to improve faculty connections. Also identify at least two faculty members that you can work with to advance your career goal.

Mentoring Lesson 6

The Mind of the Self-Directed Learner

**The world is a book and those who do not travel
read only one page.
—Augustine of Hippo**

Success Means Taking Charge

In essence, I view self-directed learning as an approach to
college requiring students to take charge of their learning
without depending solely on faculty. This is the way of the
"self-directed learner,"—pursuing learning as a collaborative
teaching-learning process between student and faculty.
Opposite of taking charge is what I view as a more passive
learning approach, or what I described earlier as a traditional
student-instructor classroom relationship. The self-directed
learner has three major attributes:

1. demonstrates an enterprising attitude,
2. applies creative thinking to get meaningful results, and
3. displays relational awareness to augment personal growth
    and educational enrichment.

Students who come to college showing initiative and a sense
of academic independence and who are self-motivated, in
my estimation, personify an enterprising attitude, which is
an important ingredient for success in today's society. The
enterprising student is willing to take difficult tasks and
confront problems and challenges head-on. He or she is able
to take risks and is quick to think outside the box.

The creative attribute of the self-directed learner is
demonstrated by a student's capacity to generate learning and
growth possibilities both within and outside of the traditional
classroom; for example, to better prepare himself or herself
for life after college. Students demonstrating this quality
take intellectual risks and aren't afraid to share thoughts of

new ideas and concepts. These students think outside of the box and are always looking for opportunities to enrich their academic life.

The relational attribute reflects the way students engage others in their educational process: other students, mentors, community leaders, business and corporate types, administrative staff, and faculty. The underlying principle of the relational aspect of self-directed learning is student recognition of the abundant opportunities from which to learn. Self-directed learning represents a shift in the way a vast number of students currently approach college. My aim is to get students to see learning as a transformational and dynamic process for which they are ultimately responsible. The level of effort and responsibility expended directly corresponds to the quality of and usefulness of the education they receive— that is, the capacity to build a solid career pathway and prepare for a productive place in today's rapidly changing economy. For example, the self-directed learner identifies and engages in extracurricular activities designed to satisfy a very specific set of academic and/or career objectives. They don't join organizations and clubs simply as an activity to put on a resume. No, absolutely not; they are essentially concerned about the creating skills building and professional growth experiences that can be accentuated in an interview.

Taking responsibility for their learning means exhibiting leadership and accountability, which is achievable when students set explicit learning goals and career objectives in their respective SWRPs, the centerpiece of the *Mentoring Handbook*. This is done by formulating personalized learning and career-development strategies. Likewise, it assumes students have explicit plans, and they're regularly monitoring the actions they take to attain specific academic and career-related outcomes.

Opening Unlocked Doors to Resources

Self-directed learners pursue learning well beyond the classroom. They draw on assistance of actors and untapped resources in the surrounding college community, creating a broader creative learning environment. So often students neglect to engage community resources and local business leaders. You would think that the doorways to the community are locked, but they are not!

Self-directed learners demonstrate the willingness to open unlocked doors. As a result, they discover rich learning opportunities beyond the walls of college that enhance their educational experience. They find unique "learning spaces" to test and apply classroom concepts to real-world situations. Over time, they heighten their awareness of the broader community as a powerful classroom in which to grow real-world skill sets and core competences.

To open unlocked doors in the community at large, my mentoring advice to new students is to set aside time in the first semester—two hours twice a week—to explore the visible and invisible resources in the community. This is an excellent way to identify unique learning opportunities, build a power social network, and locate potential internships and work experiences. Share your plans with faculty; you will be surprised at their willingness to assist in this endeavor. They might likely think of a rewarding skills building project that would give you great joy. Faculty have colleagues at neighboring schools, and are likely to know local and state government officials who are willing to have an audience with you, and have access to school administrators and local business leaders. Students, closed doors do not mean locked doors, so take the time to push on a few.

When adults know young people are trying to better themselves and make a difference, they're willing to offer opportunities to them. Sometimes, based on budget constraints, businesses can't offer paid internships to students, but I daresay many businesses or organizations would not turn down a student's request to spend a few hours a week "shadowing" employees to get a sense of what to expect when he or she joins the workforce in a particular field. And you never know when an unpaid internship might become a paid work experience based on the enthusiasm and work ethics displayed by a student.

Leadership Development Opportunities

Learning groups provide supportive environments for developing the student SWRP. By sharing the development experience, students can help and encourage each other. Faculty and other influential speakers (business leaders, local/state government officials, community advocates, and other thought-provoking leaders) are always available to serve as guest speakers and play other supportive roles.

Participating in learning groups also creates real-world leadership situations, affords students occasions to organize and manage projects, enables them to construct strong resumes, and allows them to rehearse interviewing. Keith Sawyer, associate professor of education and psychology at Washington University, has written an excellent book entitled *Group Genius: The Creative Power of Collaboration*, in which he discusses the exceptional creativity in groups. I think the book is essential reading and strongly recommend students put it on their reading lists. If need be, go in with another student to purchase a copy, or borrow the book from a classmate after he or she purchases it and reads it, but make sure you read it!

Not sure learning groups are a good idea? Take a close look at the benefits students can get from participating in peer-learning groups. In fact, peruse the list and decide whether joining a peer-learning group is something you'd want to do. Peer-learning groups

- □ cultivate healthy social lives;
- □ establish meaningful relationships with career-focused peers;
- □ provide space for exploration of ideas not covered in the classroom;
- □ encourage students to practice making presentations while honing their public speaking;
- □ allow students to practice their interview skills;
- □ help to improve writing skills;
- □ build leadership skills;

- create job-search opportunities; and
- create skill-building opportunities.

Professional Affiliations

Though joining professional organizations may not be affordable for students, the benefits are well worth the financial sacrifice. What's more, trade and professional organizations usually offer discount memberships to students. Members of peer-learning groups can split the cost of membership and take turns attending workshops and conferences. Likewise, they can share newsletters or magazines that come with paid memberships. Becoming a member of a professional organization can be instrumental when executing a job search or deciding on a career path. Associating with a professional group is also an excellent way to keep abreast of the latest information and trends in your field. By the first semester of the junior year, students should have membership in at least one professional organization or trade group.

In addition to annual conferences, students can check out workshops and seminars sponsored by professional organizations and trade associations. Also, opportunities exist for students to participate in poster contests and essay contests and in contests in which they have to present short papers. Students should make every effort to attend at least two or three professional conferences during their junior and senior years. These events present excellent opportunities to network with prominent leaders in your career field who are doing what you eventually hope to do. Oftentimes, students become aware of scholarships and internships and learn about jobs as a result of networking at conferences. So do yourself a favor and get going on finding a professional organization or trade association that meets your needs. You won't be sorry you did!

Travel Abroad Opportunities

Students should make traveling abroad an educational priority. And, if they're smart, even those who have no interest in leaving the country will learn to speak a second language because bilingual candidates are quite attractive to prospective employers. Learning a second language is especially important for students who do plan to travel, and possibly work, outside the continental United States. That's right. I said possibly work outside the United States. What once was practically unheard of is now becoming more and more commonplace as Americans work in other countries. And I'm not just talking about missionaries or physicians who work in other countries, particularly African countries. I'm talking about people in a variety of professions.

Traveling and/or working abroad can enrich students' learning and work experience and help him/her acquire vital skill sets while strengthening their resumes. It goes without saying that never before have opportunities been so readily available for young adults. Truth be told, I almost envy today's college kids because the saying "the world is your oyster," applies to them in an abundance of ways. Of course, students have to put in the work. As I said about my daughter and the other young lady I spent time interviewing, getting the opportunity to travel or work abroad isn't going to "just happen." Students have to put in the work to make travel-abroad opportunities happen. More than any other time in history, students have opportunities to live and work in communities in every corner of the global village, but they have to be willing to put in the work. (At some point during your reading, refer back to the *global skill sets* presented in Mentoring Lesson 4.)

Mentoring Lesson 7

Constructing a Resume

It's not who you are that holds you back; it's who you think you're not.
—Author unknown

The Professional Introduction Document

Whether deciding to get a job or go on to graduate school after completing college, the summary of your academic performance and work history will be reflected in a resume—what I like to refer to as a professional introduction document. In either case, your resume is one of the most important documents in your college portfolio. Its content will be analyzed, scrutinized, and dissected to determine if you are the right asset for a company or organization. What will your resume say about you?

☐ Will it adequately profile your skill sets work readiness?
☐ Will it portray an upstanding personal values system?
☐ Will it give you a unique advantage over the competition?
☐ Will your work history impress a potential employer?
☐ Will your resume get that all-important interview?

This section of the *Mentoring Handbook* gives students ideas and suggestions on how to build, organize, and write a focused resume that prospective employers will find appealing. Writing a "good" resume means understanding that its overall objective is to access interview opportunities that allow you to showcase your value to prospective employers. I remind students that the resume building and writing process starts the day you take your first class!

Making Resumes Sparkle

To make your resume sparkle, present useful information that's well-organized and properly formatted and is grammatically correct. Most importantly, take extra care to spell correctly and use accurate sentence structure. Every word written in a resume, CV, or biographical statement impacts your competitive standing among the growing ranks of job applicants. And I do mean every single word. When describing your accomplishments and work-ready attributes, make certain to use action verbs. When I reviewed resumes, one of the things that rubbed me the wrong way was the over-the-top language that students often used. Effective resumes are the ones that contain short sentences and avoid excessive use of articles and pronouns.

Remember that employers are looking for well-rounded employees who can effectively communicate verbally and in writing. According to Fran Quittel, technology and business recruiter, "companies are increasingly relying on the Internet as a way to find candidates." Further, "there are an estimated 600,000 resumes available on the Internet." A resume that sparkles is one that displays strong evidence of interpersonal relationship skills, a customer service aptitude, someone who values teamwork, exhibits an entrepreneurial spirit, and possesses executive functioning skills.

Organizing and Formatting Your Resume

A good resume is well-constructed and organized. Refer to the *Sample Resume* at the end of this lesson to get an idea of the basic components of a college resume. You will notice that at the top of the resume is the individual's contact information, including mailing address, telephone numbers, and e-mail address. It's advisable for students who are still in school to provide the address of the college or university they're attending. If you maintain a website or blog, it's suggested you list those addresses as well. But check to be certain the information on those sites doesn't pose a problem.

Next, you want to create a personal goal that's specific to the position you're seeking. To sparkle, the statement must align with the vision and mission of the company or organization. Don't know the company's vision or mission? Probably not. But a savvy job candidate will Google the company and carefully review its website to ascertain its vision or mission. A word of caution: don't get cute with your language usage. Remember, this is an opportunity to impress employers and get a leg up on the competition. Make your goal statement the template for personalizing future resumes. Next, dedicate a section to your education, followed by your work experience, which should be followed by a section on your achievements and accomplishments. Conclude with a section that lists your special training, certificates you've earned, and your hobbies.

For all intent and purpose, resumes are like personal capability statements. So, students, make sure that your resume demonstrates to prospective employers that you are capable of doing the job for which you are applying. Presenting a boring resume will put you at risk of not being taken seriously for the job. But remember that an exceptional resume alone does not guarantee a job. Other things about you will determine whether you get hired.

Practicing the tips below will help students make their resumes sparkle:

- Avoid regurgitating in your resume what you read in a job description.
- As a general rule of thumb, limit your resume to two pages unless notified otherwise.
- Refrain from going into too many details on the resume; you can toot your horn in your CV and during the job interview.
- Refrain from using vague phrases and confusing buzzwords when describing past positions and work experience.
- Highlight the pertinent events and accomplishments in your work history.
- Discuss significant organizational outcomes and/or products.
- Don't exaggerate your work duties or level of responsibility.
- Use concrete examples of your accomplishments to demonstrate job suitability.
- Resist using superfluous language and hyperbolic phrases because that will likely be perceived as grandstanding.

- Clearly state achievements and unique work experiences to grab a potential employer's attention.
- Confer with staff at your institution's Career Service Center, as well as with faculty members and your mentors, to get constructive criticism about your resume—what works and what doesn't.
- To the extent possible, "metricize" your accomplishments; for example, instead of saying that you organized and scheduled meetings for senior staff, indicate that you planned and managed an estimated number of meetings per month.
- In the case of report writing, cite the number of reports, especially error-free reports over a period of time.
- Don't exaggerate your work history or make claims that cannot be verified.

The sample resume at the end of this section gives students a basic format for developing a formal resume. My advice is that you also confer with other students and faculty for ideas. Also, go online to review sample resume formats and styles, and discuss your resume with your mentor and/or career counselor. If your resume is not telling a powerful story about you, make the appropriate modifications and/or updates. Check to see if you have overlooked any important information, or if you simply have no other noteworthy accomplishments to incorporate into your resume. If the latter is the case, I suggest that you search out work experiences and voluntary projects to fill any gaps in your resume.

Resumes Must Fit the Occasion

It's important for students not to lose sight of the occasion for which a resume is submitted. As you prepare your resumes, make certain they serve the exact purpose for which they're intended. For example, writing a resume in response to a job announcement will be different from the one crafted to accompany a letter of introduction. If a grant or fellowship is the object of the resume, it, too, is likely to be crafted differently.

Focusing on the goal and purpose for the writing of your resume will help you tailor it to fit the occasion. Some people use the same resume regardless of the situation, which is a no-no. Understanding the purpose of the resume is very important. Some companies use their own formats and structures and will often request information not asked by others employers. In any case, when preparing a resume, please be sure to consider its purpose and the occasion.

Globalizing Your Resume

Make foreign travel part of the conversation you have with your parents. Get their support and identify foreign and local travel goals in your SWRP. Be sure you share your travel plans with faculty members and mentors because they can play a major role in helping you identify travel opportunities and resources to pay for the experience. Check out well-respected educational programs offering tours to students. And don't forget about local churches, community organizations, and travel groups that sponsor group international travel. Also, visit neighboring colleges and universities to check out travel-abroad programs. The "self-directed learner" leaves no stone unturned.

Use your peer learning group to explore and share information about travel programs. The study group could conceivably partnership with a faculty member to sponsor an educational tour. How amazing would that be? Be bold and take the lead on such a project, as it may develop into an experience you'll never forget. It would definitely look fantastic on your resume.

As I conclude this section, I urge you to look for trade missions that are often sponsored by local government officials and state representatives. Step out of your comfort zone and try to negotiate a spot on the mission as a staff resource person. You never know unless you ask! So be bold and visit your congressman or senator. Plan to sit in on a legislative session or hearing. As you consider travel-abroad experiences, don't forget about the Peace Corps. I am a former Peace Corps volunteer; I had an awesome foreign travel and work experience. And I know for a fact that my having been a Peace

Corps volunteer was an attention-getter on my resume, not to mention numerous scholarship offers to major universities after my tour.

Posting an Online Digital Resume

Submit a resume to a company in response to a job announcement or an interview referral, and someone in HR will immediately Google your name. Subsequently, you need to concern yourself with the story they are likely to encounter. My advice is to check the Internet to see what personal information makes up your online professional identity. Delete any and all information that compromises your integrity or casts you in a less than stellar light. Assuming there are no issues, take the necessary actions to develop an online professional identity that builds up your personal brand. Your carefully crafted portfolio including a resume and bio-statement, and a few documents promoting your accomplishments, should be sufficient. You might also want to refer to available online applications and social media tools to assist in creating your digital portfolio.

Sample Resume

John J. Smith Jr.
123 College Street, State College, GA 12345
555-555-555 e-mail: *john.smith@school.edu*

CAREER GOAL: To earn a master's degree in marketing and create a successful advertising agency.

EDUCATION

Bachelor of Arts, Business Administration
Graduated May 2012, State College, Georgia (GPA 3.5)

WORK EXPERIENCE

- Mid-Winter Intern: December 15, 2010, to January 25, 2011
- Connors & Associates, Charlotte, NC
- Smith & Smith Enterprise, Atlanta, GA
- New Students Orientation Counselor: August 2005 and August 2006
- State College, Atlanta, GA

CAMPUS ORGANIZATIONS

- Student Government Association
- Future Business Leaders Club (Vice President)
- Kappa Delta Psi Fraternity

PROFESSIONAL ASSOCIATIONS

- National Black MBA (Student Arm)
- Junior Chamber of Commerce Club

AWARDS/RECOGNITIONS

- Dean's List throughout college
- Student of the Year (2010 and 2011)
- A. J. Smith Book Award

HOBBIES

- Skiing/Biking
- Travel
- Reading (Business History)

Writing Resume Cover Letters

Your resume should be accompanied by a strongly written cover letter that conveys information that's inappropriate for the resume. I wrote cover letters to convey two things:

1. To draw an employer's attention to the special attributes, assets, and unique skill sets that I brought to the table.
2. To assure the employer that I could help the company achieve its mission and goals.

Some people think cover letters should be straightforward. Others think it is okay to take chances in cover letters. If you're not sure which approach works best, let a faculty member read over your cover letter before you submit it. My preference has been to use a straightforward approach. The interview will provide opportunity to communicate unique insights about yourself. I do advise students to research the companies they seek interviews with, so that they are familiar their organizational mission and goals. And if probed, you can state clearly and honestly how you can help company officials achieve their mission and goals.

It is never a bad idea to get a second or third opinion on your cover letter or your resume, so share these documents with your mentors and professional associates. Of course, you can have too many cooks in the kitchen, so you don't want to just willy-nilly show it to people. But do show it to people whose opinions matter to you and who are skilled at writing good cover letters, and know what makes a prospective employer tick. I know a professional writer who charges seventy-five to fifty dollars an hour to edit resumes. She has a degree from one of the top five journalism schools in the country, and she never submits a cover letter without letting one or more of her colleagues read over it. Given the magnitude of some projects, she will send her cover letter to a team of three or more colleagues to read before submitting it.

Handling Reference Letters

Ordinarily, my advice is not to list the names of references on your resume but instead to write the obligatory sentence at the bottom of it: References available upon request. Otherwise, don't include reference letters unless they are requested. It do suggest that students list references in the CV. However, before listing individual references, be sure to get their permission. You don't want someone to get a call about you and be caught off guard. It is also important to inform your references about any job to which you're applying. If they do get a call about you, they can speak intelligently about your qualifications for the position and how you will add value to the company.

While it might be obvious to some, I will say this, nevertheless: do not ask references from individuals who cannot attest to your attributes and abilities. And finally, it is wise to present your references with copies of resumes and biographical statements to help them write an impactful reference letter or commendation for you.

Resurrecting the Biographical Statement

The biographical statement is a major tool used to present vital personal information. Bio-statements are typically used in programs to highlight the speaker, or by the person introducing the keynote speaker at a conference or lecture. They also can be used to introduce prospective candidates to employers. In the latter case, bio-statements are usually accompanied by resumes. Early in my career, I used a bio-statement to introduce myself to prospective mentors. As a coach and consultant, I'm frequently asked to supply my biographical statement. Unlike the resume, the biographical statement is written in conversational or narrative form. I always approach my bio-statement as if I'm writing a short two-page essay. The elements ordinarily covered in a biographical statement include:

name	volunteer services
family background	school activities
title	academic achievements
career objective	awards/scholarships
college	honors/awards
major area of study	unique work experience
organizations and affiliations	special training

I strongly encourage students to develop and include bio-statements in their portfolio. And it's not a bad idea to share it with faculty, counselors, and respected peers. Over the course of my career, I've used two types of biographical statements, including one with bullets that I used when I wanted people to write recommendation letters for me or to give me a reference. Many of my business associates are wedded to the bullet/consultant format, which they consider easy to read. Ordinarily I'd agree, but in the case of an employer requesting a bio-statement, I suggest a narrative format consisting of four to five paragraphs. Irrespective of the format, remember that using simple language is most effective. Also, what you write says a lot about you, so put your best foot forward!

Preparing a Curricula Vitae

The student learning and development portfolio contains information from which to construct both the resume and CV. You may recall that the resume is used primarily to communicate one's work experience in response to a particular job, to seek an introduction to a prospective employer, or to secure a job interview. The CV is a more comprehensive document containing detailed personal history. Unlike the resume, the CV is constructed using complete sentences. It uses more headings than the resume and includes a more historical description of one's educational background, employment history, specialized training, publications, licenses and certification, awards, hobbies, and affiliations.

Mentoring Lesson 8

The Work Experience Mind-Set

Internships have always been important to college students, but never more than now.
—Katie Riley

From Internships to the Mothership

Internships are excellent ways to get good work experience, find job possibilities, cultivate soft and hard workplace skills, build strong resumes, establish valuable contacts, and grow your *work-readiness portfolio*. Prospective employers look favorably upon students with internships on their resumes. Whether the internships are paid or unpaid, it's highly recommended that students participate in them each semester following their first year of college. I encourage students to make every effort to have more than three internships by the time they graduate.

Internships can be worked during the summer or in midwinter breaks. But again, don't always look for a paycheck when you get an internship. I realize you'd prefer to get paid on an internship, and that's perfectly normal, but some good internships are nonpaid. If you get a nonpaid internship, it's important for you to work just as hard on it as if you were getting paid. In fact, if you work a nonpaid internship and impress your employer with your work-readiness skills, that will stand out in your employer's mind. Certainly if you'll work hard when you're not getting paid, just imagine how hard you'll work when you are receiving a salary!

Work Opportunities Exist in Every Community

Opportunities to gain vital work experience are all around us. With a little imagination, students can create skill-building experiences with an array of social actors and business leaders in the community. For example:

- On days when your classes let out early, spend time at a local church tutoring kids in reading, writing, or math.
- Volunteer at one of the hotels in the surrounding community to assist with special events, conferences, or meetings.
- Ask the local Chamber of Commerce or other professional business associations to permit you to shadow an executive staff member.
- Organize a peer study group to plan and organize campus-based seminars and workshops to discuss academic and career-related issues of mutual interest to students. Topics should include how to study, interview techniques, how to write resumes, how to design and launch job searches, and how to find an internship.

These are just a few examples of what self-directed learners can accomplish with a little imagination. And this is the stuff of which great resumes are made. Trust me, prospective employers will find these kinds of students very appealing. It's true this will require you to expend a little energy organizing meetings and stepping out of your comfort zone to talk to people. But just think of all of the potential benefits! Besides, being able to craft an attention-grabbing resume allows you to build confidence, learn how to negotiate, improve your communication skills, and manage projects. Again, take advantage of faculty and administrative staff that are on hand to assist you. They know community people who can direct you to places in and around the campus where you can find some value-added work experiences.

Making Work Experiences Count

When looking for an internship or summer work, focus on your career path. You want work experience that helps satisfy your career objective. Find out about the company—its vision and its mission. Go to the company's website, peruse the list of staff, and then select someone to call. Let that person know you're interested in working there and inquire whether you can ask a few questions about the company. For instance, you may want to ask whether the company has a casual attire dress code on Fridays. If you're fortunate to reach someone who's willing to speak to you, make sure you use your time wisely and ask good questions. Spend time thinking about what you can get from the experience, should you land an internship there. Also, think about what you can bring to the company—or bring to the table, as people like to say. You may also ask whether the work permits you to practice information and theories learned in the classroom.

Avoid internships that lack structured procedures and protocols because you could end up being a gofer. In other words, you could end up being the person who has to make the morning coffee run, or the person who has to hang back to answer the phones when everybody else goes out to lunch to celebrate the new supervisor's birthday. Gofer positions offer very much in the way of practical learning experience, and, at the end of the summer, you could find yourself scratching your head and wondering why you wasted your time. What you most want to get from internships is practical experience that will help you down the road in your career, and strengthen your chances for having a good, satisfying career. Also, making good use of internships will likely give you an advantage in the job applicant pool. So make good choices and bring your A game.

Internships Produce Big Benefits

Students are encouraged to take a close look at the benefits below that can be obtained from an internship or community service. The list can be used to establish the merit of a particular work experience and can also serve as a guide for setting personal internship or work-experience goals.

□ Augment learning and personal development
□ Build leadership skills
□ Strengthen interpersonal skills
□ Enhance professional and technical knowledge
□ Provide vital input for the student portfolio
□ Obtain experience to put on your resumes and CVs
□ Lead to publishing and public speaking opportunities
□ Strengthen oral and written communication skills
□ Build powerful career-oriented social networks

☐ Acquire reference letters and commendations
☐ Provide access to rich mentoring/coaching experiences

Interviewing for Internships, Etc.

When interviewing for internships, don't be intimidated. Remember to ask important questions and remember to take a second or two to think about your responses before you start speaking. Talk to people who interned at the company in the past to learn information that may be valuable to you. For example, they could talk to you about the culture and the climate at the company—the dos and don'ts of the organization. If you're applying for a specific position, ask the person who's interviewing you to describe, in detail, your duties and responsibilities. Also ask for a written statement of the tasks you will be expected to perform. If you get the internship, make sure you confirm your work schedule, including days and hours. As an intern, it's important for you to familiarize yourself with the dos and don'ts below:

☐ Never leave work right at quitting time. Hang around a little past five—or whatever time you're supposed to get off—and ask one of the full-time staffers whether there's anything you can help him or her do. Not being anxious to dash out the door will make a good impression on your coworkers.
☐ Request that you be assigned a supervisor. Also ask someone to mentor you during the summer. (These are two different people.)
☐ Before the internship ends, ask for a written evaluation of your work experience on company letterhead.
☐ Discuss your expectations and career goals up front with your supervisor and mentor to ensure you have a quality internship.

How to Exit an Internship

Make the internship memorable: meet people, make an impression, and complete a signature work task or project! Before your last day, write a short note to thank the people who were instrumental in helping you during your internship:

thank them for their guidance and the exceptional growth experience; and state how the internship benefited you and helped you to grow.

Write special thank-you notes to your mentor, your supervisor, and the head of the company, and don't forget to offer a word to the administrative assistant. Don't forget about any professors or staff people at your institution who gave you good advice before you went on your interview for the internship. Thank-you notes don't cost much, and writing them won't take long, but they can and often do make lasting impressions on people. Think of it this way. Let's say you and the other intern performed equally well, and you both have great GPAs. If the company has to make budget cuts and goes from two interns to one next year, the thank-you notes you hand out at the end of the internship might be what gets you invited back.

But guess what? Even when you don't get the internship, you should write thank-you notes to the people with whom you interviewed. In your note, let them know you appreciate the opportunity to interview for the position. Ask if they'd be amenable to telling you what you can do in the future to better your chances of being chosen next time. Also, ask whether they know of any other internship possibilities you may want to explore. Don't play small; take charge of your career. In the process, you will meet influential people and make lasting friendships.

Journal Your Internship Experiences

Make it a practice to use a journal to record your internship and other work experiences. This is a useful tool for recording major accomplishments, your involvement in significant activities, problem-solving experiences, significant meetings and conferences, and major career contacts. Carry the journal with you to interviews, and when the occasion presents itself, present it to showcase your creativity and your self-evaluation skills. The notes and comments contained in the journal will become useful information when preparing and rehearsing for interviews.

Mentoring Lesson 9

Interviewing with Confidence

**The best way to predict the future is to create it.
—Abraham Lincoln**

Factors Making for a Favorable Interview

Interview readiness is one of the most important factors in the job-search process. It might surprise some readers, but based on my work history and HR experience, I know for a fact that a good interview can sometimes get more results than a good resume. Oftentimes, and I say this with unequivocal confidence, the person with the best resume does not always get the job. Therefore, a brief discussion on the interview process is in order. But before we get started, please take a moment to peruse factors that can assist you in having favorable outcomes after your interview.

- Having solid knowledge of your career field
- Career-specific social networking
- Asking mentors and coaches to prepare you on how to navigate the interview process
- Attending job fairs and participating in conferences and seminars
- Scheduling as many interviews as you can reasonably handle

My professional career spans nearly four decades, and during that time I've accumulated considerable firsthand experience and knowledge about the dynamics of the interview process. Selecting personnel for key staff positions, evaluating and selecting contractors, writing tons of position descriptions, and selecting candidates for overseas assignments have afforded me the opportunity to build a substantial body of knowledge on a range of interview methods. An overview of what I consider five common types of interview methods that students are likely to encounter is presented at the end of this lesson. Exposure to these five formats will prove to be an immense benefit to students.

I do urge students to purchase a few books on interviewing techniques. The more prepared you are when you arrive for an interview, the more likely you are to get the job offer. Information gained from a few good books will prepare you to interview successfully, regardless of the methods used by prospective employers. In the meantime, I offer relevant strategies and insights in this lesson that will help students experience favorable interview outcomes.

Journal Interview Lessons Learned

A smart way to develop great interview skills and confidence is to journal your interview experience. After each interview, list what you consider to be the strong points and the weak points that occurred during the interview. Also, write about how you felt during and after the interview. Reflect on questions for which you were well-prepared to answer, and those areas you e must strengthen in future interviews. Of course, you won't be the one calling the shots, the one asking the questions during the interview, but you should be savvy enough to find a way to discuss whatever it is you know you're good at discussing. Take mental notes during the interview; then, after it's over, whip out your journal and record and analyze your sentiments and observations. In interviews, I always asked job applicants about the most recent book they had read. I did that because I really didn't want to hire anybody who didn't take time to read, and I also found it fascinating to learn just what types of books people were into.

Strengthen your interview confidence by taking a moment to peruse these additional thoughts on interview journaling.

☐ Make sure you know the purpose of an interview and prepare accordingly. For example, if you have been granted a courtesy interview by virtue of a friend or associate, know for certain whether it's for a job referral, reference letter, or a contact. The point is to plan for and rehearse the interview.

- Take time to learn about the organization or company interviewing you to make sure you're a reasonable "fit" in their workplace culture. This is important as you try to determine whether you'd be able to make a reasonable contribution to the company's goals.
- When arriving at and walking through the interview site, observe the physical characteristics of the workplace and the demeanor of the workers. How people are behaving can be very revealing about the culture and climate of the workplace.
- Observe the conduct of staff and how the interviewer prepares for the interview. Observe the manners of the interviewer and how you are greeted. Notice whether the interviewer is on time. Were the questions well-thought-out and presented in a systematic way?
- It bears repeating that you should buy a few books on interviewing to read, and you should also search the Internet for suggestions and ideas on how to create a results-oriented interview.

In today's fast-paced world, many job seekers skip creating the perfect introduction. But when competition for every job is intense, a cover letter can make a strong first impression and help an applicant stand out in the crowd. In the newest edition of his bestselling text, Martin Yate discusses in detail the types of cover letters that will make good impressions on a prospective employer. Other authors are equally talented in sharing the art form and science of effective interviewing. By working in peer-learning groups, students are able to share the costs of buying multiple books to build their interview intelligence and confidence. Peer group participants can role-play in mock interviews and help each other prepare for actual job interviews.

Getting Noticed

If students want employers to notice them, they'll have to create effective interview documents: resumes, bio-statements, and resume cover letters. To help students understand and successfully navigate the interview process, the author has paid considerable attention to this section. In light of ever-changing marketplace realities and new demands from a changing educational landscape, students must heed these instructions. Today companies are inundated with resumes from students from around globe. They look at thousands of applications from eager students and from workers making career changes. Your documents will get noticed only if they are clearly written and cutting-edge. To help students get that competitive edge, I've identified five books on interviewing that you'll find instructive and informative:

□ *The 250 Job Interview Questions You'll Most Likely Be Asked … And the Answers that Will Get you Hired*—Peter Veruki
□ *Best Answers to the 201 Most Frequently Asked Interview Questions*—Matthew J. DeLuca
□ *Interviewing: Master the Moment That Gets You the Job*—Jeffrey Taylor and Doug Hardy (Monster Careers)
□ *Knock 'Em Dead Job Interview: How to Turn Job Interviews into Job Offers*—Martin Yate
□ *Knock 'Em Dead Cover Letters: Great Letter Techniques and Samples for Every Step of Your Job Search*, Martin Yate

Any of the books featured above will give students tremendous insight on the job-search process, how to write the most effective resumes and CVs, and the best strategies for negotiating salaries. Martin Yate's book does an excellent job of informing job hunters of some of the tough interview questions that are often asked by employers. For example:

□ Why should I hire you?
□ What are your outstanding qualities?
□ Why do you want to work for my company?
□ What is your greatest weakness?
□ How much money do you want?

Reading one or more of these books will prepare students to tackle tough interview questions and make good impressions. Journaling the frequently asked questions during interviews, rehearsing your answers, and seeking practice interviews are great ways to create a unique advantage in the future interviews. Students can begin rehearsing by writing answers to the five aforementioned questions, which I deem to be the most challenging for the best and brightest job seekers.

Common Interview Methods

Traditional Interview. As a supervisor with hiring responsibilities, early on in my career I followed the traditional interview format, which consisted of asking a range of questions to assess one's skills, knowledge, and abilities and to verify information presented on an application or in the CV and/or resume. This approach was more conversational in practice. Over the years, however, I realized this interview format is only as effective as the individual asking the questions. So pay close attention to the confidence level of the interviewer and the questions you're asked because a skilled interviewee can exploit this. A less-than-skilled interviewer will do a poor job assessing a candidate's qualifications and accomplishments using the traditional interview format. One reason this is likely to happen is that the questions are not uniformed, and are sometimes not well thought out. Consequently, comparing job applicants can be problematic. Today, however, managers are more inclined to use structured versions of the traditional interview format—each applicant is asked the same set of questions. In today's competitive market, applicants are likely to encounter prospective employers who use more vigorous interview techniques to hire the best person for a job.

Behavioral-Oriented Interview. With a strong focus on building individual and organizational capacity, managers find that "behavioral interviewing techniques" are an effective way to screen job applicants. Many companies find that using a behavior-based interview format reveals the best and brightest talent. In this interview approach, litanies of carefully structured questions are asked to conduct a rather detailed assessment of an applicant's past job performance. This method places a heavy emphasis on gathering information on competency, executive functioning skills, job knowledge, and one's future value to an organization.

Job seekers encountering the behavioral-based interview method are expected to provide real-world examples from past work experiences: writing and verbal communication skills, problem-solving experiences, conflict resolution, workplace politics, interpersonal issues, leadership and management issues, teamwork, and the ability to adapt to change. Essentially, job applicants must share evidenced-based responses to interviewer's questions.

Mixed Traditional and Behavioral Interview. Later in my career, my colleagues and I relied on a mixed version of the traditional and behavior-oriented interview format to evaluate a candidate's qualifications and accomplishments. Candidates would be asked the same set of questions by a single interviewer or a group of interviewers to enable making the most informed selection. I refer to this method as a "directed interview method" because it falls into the category of a "structured interview" format.

The Group/Panel Interview Method. The group interview involves several interviewers who seek to get a better picture of the job applicant simultaneously. In other words, you might be in a room with as many as eight to ten people who take turns asking you questions. This method is used to assess an applicant's presentation skills, ability to communicate, knowledge of the company, and level of interest in a company. It can be daunting for some people. In an age when teamwork has become the norm in the workplace, the group/panel interview is often the method of choice. Group/panel interviews are also reflective of a company's participatory management practices.

Audition Type Interview. Many employers make considerable use of the audition interview. In this scenario, an interviewer, or several interviewers, will have a candidate perform a particular exercise. For example, a technical writer might be asked to produce an impromptu writing sample. A candidate applying for an administrative assistant position might be asked to demonstrate keyboarding skills. A graphic artist could be tasked to demonstrate his or her skills through an interactive design exercise.

The Screening Interview. Screening interviews are generally performed by companies to determine whether an applicant meets the qualifications of a particular position. The individual conducting the interview focuses on identifying and explaining gaps in an applicant's employment history. The primary objective of the screening method is to verify reported credentials and explain inconsistencies stated in the resume, application, or college transcript. The goal of this interview approach is to produce a panel of qualified applicants. Nowadays, many screening interviews are done over the phone.

Student Alert. Motivated by the need to hire candidates who will make the best contribution to a company's mission, employers are devising a number of creative ways to conduct job interviews. Recently a young associate shared with me that she was part of a group interview that consisted of five interviewers and three job applicants. She ended up getting the job. When asked why she thought she was selected, the response was, "I did not show one iota of fear; I was confident throughout the process. I was concise in my responses to questions and had two or three good questions that I asked the interviewers. My countless interview rehearsals, journal notes, and the informational interviews I participated in prepared me well."

The Informational Interview

I became acquainted with the concept of the informational interview in a career-development workshop decades ago. Sadly, I hear too few people talking about or making use of this valuable tool today. The concept was one of many career-development principles introduced in Richard Bolles's *What Color is Your Parachute: Guide to Rethinking Interviews.* The book has undergone significant revision and is even more popular today. Students should get a copy for their library and make it a close companion.

Unlike a regular job interview, the informational interview is initiated by an individual seeking information about a company and not by an employer evaluating a potential candidate. Informational interviews involve meeting with and talking to people in various fields and industries to obtain useful information and gain career insights. Conducting an informational interview is a practical way to learn about a company and industry trends in a career field. Stories abound about individuals who bitterly lament accepting a job offer before properly vetting a company or organization. By the same token, informational interviews have enabled students to gain valuable contacts and employment leads. Informational interviews provide awesome opportunities for building a social network, a critical component of an effective job search in today's society.

The Power of the Informational Interview

The empowering effects of the *"informational interview"* cannot be overlooked by students. In a recent conversation with a colleague who's an executive coach, I was reminded of some startling statistics. According to this colleague, "one in twelve informational interviews is likely to produce a job, whereas only one single job might result from sending out two hundred or more resumes."

The informational interview is also a great way to solicit letters of recommendation and to locate mentors. Getting tips about job opportunities, which are often unpublished and unannounced, is another great benefit of an informational interview. My advice to students is to schedule and participate in a minimum of two informational interviews each semester following the freshman year. Remember, it's never too early to start practicing your interview skills.

Gaining knowledge through an informational interview not only gives insights to problems and challenges facing a company or organization, but it also allows students to assess their skill sets and technical knowledge. After an interview— informal or otherwise—always handwrite a thank-you letter. Take the opportunity in your letter to include a few sentences on how you might assist in solving a particular problem or a challenge articulated by an employer during the interview. That will undoubtedly impress the person to whom the letter is addressed, and it will show you were paying attention in the interview. (Believe it or not, some people don't pay attention in interviews as well as you might think they should.)

The Hidden Job Market

In my very first informational interview, I learned about the hidden job market, which does exist. According to Jessica Dickler (*CCNMoney*—June 10, 2009) many job openings aren't advertised; therefore, job applicants have to be resourceful in finding them. Howard Poplinger, owner of human resource company Epic Development and Evaluation, says that "over eighty percent of today's jobs aren't advertised." For a number of reasons, employers don't always advertise jobs in classified ads, professional journals, or online. In casual conversations with business associates and friends in the human resource field, I've been told employers are reluctant to deal with the ever-increasing number of job seekers applying for openings. Nowadays, it's not uncommon to have two hundred applicants for one position.

I was recently reminded by a business acquaintance that his company relied strictly on employee networks for job referrals. Using the employee network saves companies money and time by bypassing traditional advertising. That employers in today's job market are depending on their workers for job referrals is further proof of the value of building strong social networks. The student job search should therefore include engaging well-positioned people in a company or organization in conversation. Remember, companies are always looking to hire well-qualified people, so treat every conversation with a prospective employer as an opportunity for a job offer.

Scheduling Informational Interviews

Social networking is the principle source for discovering and setting up informational interviews. Identifying business leaders and accomplished individuals in one's chosen career field provides fertile ground for accessing informational interviews. Conferences and professional journals are other sources to consider. As the initiator, the student takes ownership and control of the interview, deciding what information is needed and what questions to ask. The more informational interviews you do, the more your confidence will grow. Likewise, you will enhance your comfort level when you communicate with potential employers. I assure you that prospective employers will find a confident job applicant impressive, and they'll be eager to make that person part of their team.

The Job Search Is a Planned Activity

Contrary to what many students believe or practice, a job search is not simply a reaction to posted ads, or a process that starts during one's senior year. Aligning academic performance and career aspirations in the freshman year, in reality, lays the foundation for a successful job search plan. As I have asserted repeatedly, building employability potential is the ultimate goal of college. Fail to take this approach, and you will most likely end up after graduation just reacting to posted online job ads and vacancy announcements listed in professional journals. It is not my objective to minimize these potential sources of employment; they can generate interesting referrals and important job contacts. I simply don't want students to wait until graduation to start the job search process.

Building a stellar resume, learning to write attention-getting cover letters, and building a power social network are several major activities addressed in your SWRP during college. So in reality, the job search process starts as students begin taking classes. This is the time to begin exploring career pathways and building job readiness capacity, which means acquiring the requisite skill sets to succeed in the workplace. Once again, a major assumption of this *Mentoring Handbook* is that individuals primarily attend college to enhance their employability potential. First, they spend money in hopes of making money, and after graduation they want to secure a substantial-paying job in a career field of their choice. Second, another underlying supposition is that all students can graduate from college fully prepared to get a job. Third, a strong job search campaign starts with developing a SWRP, which is the basis for preparing and presenting a polished resume.

I want students to explore online and journal employment opportunities, an activity suggested in developing their *SWRP*. As part of their job search strategy, students are encouraged to "drill down" into company profiles to learn as much as they can about them: the type of professionals hired, business and industry trends, hiring policies, training and professional development opportunities, and potential contacts. Over the course of four years, a student can assemble an incredible database. The smart student, and classmates working with a peer leaning group, will have an awesome advantage over the competition.

When starting your job search, make sure to have quality stationery, matching envelopes, and stamps. I read recently that "hand-written addressed envelopes are more likely to reach hiring managers' desks than typed-addressed envelopes from non-clients or vendors." Be mindful of job-search etiquette with follow-up and thank-you letters. Also, establish e-mail accounts, properly format e-mail messages, schedule appointments, request referrals, ask for reference letters, and try to avoid missing appointments and/or being tardy.

Remember, the job search starts the day you arrive on campus.

Everything you do from that moment will shape your capacity to execute a results-oriented job search. Of course, you'll devote more serious attention and thought to your job search during your junior and senior years, but don't squander opportunities to begin working on it during your freshman and sophomore years. Take time to study the *job-search protocol* presented to students at the end of this mentoring lesson.

Job-Search Protocol

1. **Organize your job search.**

- Schedule time to execute your search.
- Use the weekend to carry out search activities.

2. **Construct a job-search filing system.**

   - Set up a manual or computer-based file and keep copies of the various materials and documents you'll generate to support your job search.
   - Make additions to and modify your portfolio as appropriate.
   - Journalize the job search experience and review your actions periodically.

3. **Produce a standard professional and polished resume.**

   - Use the standard resume for job fairs, introductions, and basic referrals.
   - Be prepared to customize your standard resume to fit jobs of interest to you.

4. **Prepare a boiler-plate resume cover letter that you can customize as needed.**

5. **Determine the kind of position you want.**

   - Target potential employers and companies in your field.
   - Seek informal interviews and referrals.
   - Determine a weekly number of resumes you'll send and stick to it.
   - Schedule and participate in a discrete number of informal and practice interviews each week.
   - Locate and go to job fairs.

6. **Schedule and conduct informational interviews.**

   - Learn from people doing the job you want to do.
   - Identify the skills needed to succeed in your field.
   - Get a professional's perspective on your qualifications.
   - Expand your social and career networks.
   - Identify career trends and future job opportunities in your field.

7. **Look for online career sites to which to post your resume.**

   - Consider creating LinkedIn and Twitter profiles.
   - Conduct a search of professional journals and trade magazines.

8. **Crank up your social and career networks.**

   - Identify individuals with whom to share your qualifications/resume.
   - Allocate a good bit of time to social networking.
   - Inform network actors that you're job hunting.
   - Plan a networking party with other job seekers to share ideas and leads.

9. **Build a personal brand.**

   - Create a professional image.
   - Be quick to follow up on responses to your inquiries.
   - Send thank-you notes to companies you contact.

10. **Solicit reference and recommendation letters.**

Mentoring Lesson 10

Making Contacts Count

If you look at history, innovation doesn't come just from giving people incentives; it comes from creating environments where their ideas can connect.
—Steven Johnson

Leveraging Relationships

Untapped assets and talents are buried in every network, the very foundation on which blessings flow. The trouble is that most of us never fully appreciate the networks we have but instead see the people we know as disparate units.

Students fail to see people in terms of strategic alliances with unlimited possibilities. I want to change that perspective and also get students to realize that their social networks extend way beyond the technology they hold in the palms of their hands. In other words, don't just use your iPhone to send senseless tweets or to go to your Facebook page to see what your friends have posted.

College is a great time to optimize and leverage personal contacts. So take advantage of every opportunity to enhance personal interactions and develop a directory of contacts. This practical tool is an excellent way to track and mange important business contacts. A simple way to do this is to use three-by-five cards or software to capture the following information. The sample format below will prove useful for developing social network profiles on influential individuals that can most likely play a role in helping you achieve your career and life goals.

Name of Contact: _____ **Title:** _____

Job/Career Field: _____

Name of Organization: _____

Mailing Address: _____

Office No.: _____ **Cell No.** _____

E-mail Address: _____

Building a Power Social Network

Social networking is an important career-building tool. It is imperative that students learn the value of social networking in creating career pathways. In college, it starts with faculty interactions and participation in student organizations, and it also includes attending professional conferences, joining the student wing of professional associations, and practicing informational interviews. Subscribing to professional journals and business-related periodicals are also opportunities for identifying and meeting influential people. Attending job fairs is another excellent way for students to make lasting contacts.

Don't be afraid to contact the people you read about in journals, industry press releases, or see on the news. Start making use of those business cards you have been collecting. And please know it's perfectly acceptable to send these contacts letters or e-mails to seek career advice. Trust me, these individuals are more than happy to give you advice, serve as a mentor, and make referrals to their friends and business colleagues. In fact, most of them will embrace the chance to help out a young person who's trying to get on the right career path. In fact, if they're honest, they'd probably be downright flattered that you thought enough of them to seek their help or advice.

Networking Tools and Actors

With the marriage of communication technology and knowledge-management application**s**, computer-driven social networking is becoming very popular. Interestingly enough, however, individuals engaging in social networking approach the network in pretty much the same way. What I mean is that they tend to exhibit a single-mindedness of purpose and echo a self-centered theme of "what's in it for me." And, as a result of being rooted in self-serving agendas, they remain oblivious to the human capital inherent in network. Another significant shortcoming of today's network actors is their failed spiritual recognition that they are catalytic agents who have the awesome potential to transform the lives of others.

Mining Network Assets

Over the years I've built a social network model that I want to share with students. In particular, I want students to understand the spiritual dimension of networking and the blessings and wealth of information that flow through networks. My aim is to help students discover and capitalize on the rich talent and assets in the universal house of human relationships.

Practically all college students are engaged in some form of social networking, but when asked to define the term, many of them struggle to come up with a definition. What they're likely to mention is social media technology. To best understand what a social network is, we have only to look at human society. What we see is that human society is composed of many social relationships—both formal and informal. These relationships stem from professional associations, family and friendship groups, and other activities and events that unite people. As we meet people in various social settings, we gain access to contacts that can assist us in many ways. But the extent and value of these contacts won't be realized unless the actors engage with one another.

A skilled social networker seeks to cultivate as many relationships with as many people as possible. He or she realizes that every contact is connected to other networks. They know that behind every contact or business card is a unique personal story and a vision that can touch the life of another network actor. Engaging other network actors is the spiritual essence of the social network. Conservatively speaking, each of us on an average knows an estimated 250 people, and each of those 250 people know 250 people. Get my drift? Do the math!

Social Networks and the Job Search

A power social network is the single most effective job search strategy a student can have after completing college. Though opting to attend graduate school after graduation, I did receive a job offer as a result of a mentor relationship. In fact, every job I've ever had over the course of four decades was a result of a referral from a friend or a business associate. So my advice to students is to make social networking a top priority. First of all, a well-functioning social network will minimize the pressures of looking for a job. Start with the individuals around you; failing to take advantage of contacts right at your fingertips is a huge career mistake.

I do not consider today's incessant use of social media as a form of social networking. In my estimation, Facebook, Twitter, LinkedIn, and the rest are just tools. They can get you started, but real social networking is a process of gathering and mining data from the contact directories and social network profiles that you generate over time.

Behind Every Business Card Is a Social Network

I want to take a little time at this point to make a few salient points about business cards. Presenting and accepting business cards is a common practice, and is a basic step in initiating power social networks. Business cards connect people to great information, ideas, job opportunities, and power networks. Seldom do I leave home without a stack of business cards in my pocket. Invariably, I find myself in a conversation where someone will ask if I have a business card. Sharing a card at that moment, instead looking for pen and paper to write down my contact information, creates an impression of professionalism. Moreover, the individual requesting the card has some idea of who I am and what I do.

Sharing a business card is an invitation to a follow-up—the beginning of actual networking. Merely accepting a business card is not networking; it's just a tool that enables one to initiate the networking process. A responsible networker (1) gets to know the individuals who shared their business cards; and (2) stays in touch with them, and whenever occasion presents itself, reaches out with a call or a short note. Most interestingly, a responsible networker recognizes that a business card represents a doorway to power networks that can help you, as well as enable you to help other people.

It is reasonable to assume that many students collect business cards from individuals visiting their campus for various programs and activities. And, of course, there are other networking occasions for them to request business cards from people. I am going to further assume that students very seldom do anything with those cards. Well, I want to encourage you to make use of the business cards that you have been fortunate to obtain. Don't file them away or toss them aside. Make it a practice to contact the individual who shared his/her card with you. When I am asked for a business card, my expectation is that the person requesting the card will contact me. Otherwise, why request someone's business card?

Following up on a business card is a sure way to create a memorable impression on someone. This individual could give you vital career advice, make critical referrals to other associates, and/or direct you to potential job offers. Let me make it clear to you: transitioning from college to the world of work is a function of knowing and investing in other people. In the final analysis, regardless of your stellar GPA, unique skills and core competences, your career field, or your charming personality, you will need people to get that job interview. And it will be people who will give that recommendation or write the reference that persuades some prospective employer to hire you instead of another job applicant.

The Student Business Card

Transitioning from college to the world of work is a function of knowing and investing in people, so I encourage every student to have a business card in his/her possession. Wherever there are people, you have a networking opportunity! Computer-generated business cards are easy to crank out, so get busy and create thirty or forty cards and be ready to introduce yourself to people. Don't be shy! That student business card you generated by computer or purchased is a basic tool to start building your network. Despite your stellar GPA, a charming personality, or unique skill sets, you need people to get a job.

As you think about your business cards, focus on making them readable and error free. Do not spend a lot of time creating slick business cards with a bunch of creative designs. Those on the receiving end are likely to find such cards far too elaborate and overdone. Once the first job is secured, there will be plenty of time to design an attractive business card that reflects a marketing theme. For now, consider the sample student business card provided below.

> **John/Mary Doe**
> **Student**
> **Business Administration Major**
> **Smart College**
> **Success, North Carolina**
> **555-111-0000**
> **Jmdoe000@yahoo.com**

Social Network Functionality Inventory

Students are urged to take a few minutes to complete the Social Network Functionality Inventory at the end of this mentoring lesson. This tool is designed to assess a student's level of network functionality, or a student's effectiveness as a network actor and architect. The inventory also will help students set growth goals and develop a network-engagement agenda to expand personal contacts and orchestrate more purpose-driven, career-related networking. I invite students to take a few minutes to complete the inventory to gauge their networking capacity. You might find the results enlightening. Each statement in the inventory is followed by a scale numbered 1 through 5. Simply read the statement and circle the number that reflects your personal assessment.

The value scale is as follows: **1**—Never, **2**—Rarely, **3**—Sometimes, **4**—Very Often, and **5**—Always. Once the inventory is completed, add the scores. The final score is the sum of the ratings for all of the items circled. After you have added the scores, divide the sum by ten, and that number will represent the *Inventory Functionality Value* (IFV). To interpret your IFV score, use the following criteria:

☐ Zero to twenty = mediocre network functionality
☐ Twenty-one to forty = low network functionality
☐ Forty-one to sixty = good network functionality
☐ Sixty-one to eighty = excellent network functionality
☐ Eighty-one to one hundred = exceptional network functionality

This scale is merely a tool to get a basic assessment of one's level of network-engagement capacity. Though not a field-tested scientific survey instrument, it does serve to help students gauge their networking functionality and what they can do to improve their social networking skills. For example, a score under forty might suggest that a student is socially inhibited.

The Universality of Social Networking

Social networking is a universal principle. Accordingly, it is incumbent on students in the new global landscape to create, manage, and sustain quality human relationships, the very essence of the individual and collective bio-dramas we call life. I offer for consideration the following principals of Universal Social Networking.

☐ Social networks are the vehicles for delivering blessings.
☐ Social networks are rich in human capital and personal assets.
☐ Social networks are building blocks for success.

☐ Social networks connect influential and empowered leaders.

Over the course of my career, I've observed how social networks can play a major role in helping individuals to achieve their goals, as well as help others to enjoy life-changing experiences. Connecting with and engaging "network actors" creates rich experiences that can lead to unbelievable assets and possibilities. As you begin to build and harvest network assets, possibilities will begin to unfold right before your eyes. You will also realize the influence you can have in helping to shape the future of others. And believe me, when you get to that point where you're helping to shape others' futures, you'll get it. You'll realize that's what we're here for: to help others, to be of service, and to be a blessing to people.

Cultivating and Managing Contacts

Networking is a lifelong process of making and managing relationships. In the beginning of this section, I asserted that untapped assets and talents are buried in every network. This is true, but the vast majority of people seldom enjoy the treasure trove of assets and talents in their reach because they lack basic knowledge of the relational underpinnings of social networks. Basically, this means knowing the needs of your network actors and how they can help you. Also, it's letting the actors know what you are doing and what new contacts you've made.

Knowing people's needs and interests affords an individual with opportunities to connect them to other people with similar interests. It is through these boundless network connections that networkers are able to share their respective knowledge and talents. Hence, giving back is a very important principle of effective social networking, and is a key relational underpinning. As people respond to the problems and requests for assistance from various network actors, several things happen, which usually go unnoticed. For one, expanded alliances and relationships will be formed with members from other networks, widening and enriching networks with new talents and assets. The net effect is access to multiple networks, which translates into a far-reaching web of social influence that can impact helping job seekers get a job or an interview.

Creating Encounter Agendas

In addition to the *Social Network Functionality Inventory*, students are urged to create and make use of an "Encounter Agenda." This is simply an outline of the topics you want to discuss with individuals in advance of planned visits and telephone inquiries. The basic idea of an encounter agenda is to direct the conversation to ensure that you address your specific concerns and interests. The encounter agenda is a tool to assist you in journaling and managing social network encounters. Planning and scheduling interviews, routine meetings, and interaction with a mentor are all ideal situations for preparing and using encounter agendas.

This is an excellent tool for conducting an encounter in a coherent and professional manner. It is also a great way to strengthen confidence and to assert yourself. Students are referred to the example below to get a sense of how a basic encounter agenda is constructed on a single sheet of paper.

Encounter Contact Agenda

Encounter: Meeting /__/ Interview /__/ Referral /__/ Other /__/

Date of Encounter: _____Time of Encounter: _____

Purpose of the Encounter:

Name of Individual (s):

Organization:

Topics Covered:

Referrals/Contacts):

Lessons Learned:

Social Network Functionality Inventory

1. I treat all my relationships and contacts as my network.
   1   2   3   4   5

2. I intentionally connect network members around their common goals and interests.
   1   2   3   4   5

3. My contacts are aware of my social networking efforts.
   1   2   3   4   5

4. I have some sense of the network members who are people of power, position, and influence.
   1   2   3   4   5

5. I maintain profiles on the network participants.
   1   2   3   4   5

6. I share profile information with other members of my network.
   1   2   3   4   5

7. I use my profile information to make meaningful connections.
   1   2   3   4   5

8. Various strategies are used to feed the network.
   1   2   3   4   5

9. I recognize the "spiritual character" of social networks.
   1   2   3   4   5

10. My motivation for networking includes creating opportunities for other people as well as for myself.
    1   2   3   4   5

Mentoring Lesson 11

Establishing Mentoring Relationships

**If you cannot see where you are going, ask someone
who has been there before.
—J. Loren Norris**

Finding the Right Mentor

The *Mentoring Handbook* sees a mentor as an individual who
is available to listen and give advice to a student on a range
of topics—not just about college but life in general. The most
effective mentor-mentee relationships, formal or informal, are
driven by specific academic and career/performance-related
objectives. A student-mentor relationship may or may not
culminate into a long-term relationship, but students should
make every effort to sustain productive mentor relationships.

Every student should have a mentor, preferably someone in
his/her career field—or what I call a career mentor. Strangely
enough, as much talk as we hear about the value of mentoring,
so few people, especially young college students, take
advantage of establishing effective mentoring relationships.
Mentors are a source of encouragement and inspiration,
and they can expose students to incredible personal-growth
experiences. In addition to helping students shape their career
pathways, mentors can help students diagnose a potential
employer's political and social culture. This information is
critical when preparing for interviews and making decisions
about job offers.

Protocol for Finding a Mentor

Students who are having challenges establishing a mentor
relationship might want to consider the nine suggested steps
listed on the following page. As was suggested in the section
on building social networks, look to professional associations,
the business community, your church or faith community,

and your system of referrals to identify potential mentors. One way to jump-start the mentor quest is to ask a faculty member to formally introduce you to a likely candidate. As you pursue your quest for a mentor, remember that shared respect and mutual trust form the foundation of a strong and productive student-mentor relationship.

Don't forget about family members and family friends who can also make referrals for you. Students are encouraged to review the eight steps for guidance on establishing a trusting and productive mentor-mentee relationship.

1. Formulate a clear idea of what kind of help you want from a mentor.
2. Express your needs in writing.
3. Confer with faculty and staff to identify three to five individuals who might be willing to serve as a mentor for you.
4. Get the contact information of the named individuals and write and/or call them.
5. Seek resumes from the positive responses and review them with the assistance of fellow students and/or faculty.
6. Make your decision and provide the prospective mentor with a bio-statement.
7. Make sure to share your academic and career goals.
8. Connect on the telephone or through e-mail, or have a face-to-face talk to confirm a social contract.

Behavior of the Self-Directed Learner

Define career field: To maximize precious study and career preparation time, it's important for students declare and concentrate on a specific area of study in the freshman year of college. Think about your end goal and get busy becoming that professional type.

Identify a faculty mentor: Confer with faculty to get help in crafting a course of study that best prepares you for your field of choice and increases your access to certain jobs in that field.

Identify a career mentor: Identify a career mentor who can help you in your career choices and guide you through an uncertain job market.

Visit a career counselor: Establish and sustain a good relationship with your career counseling office.

Start an academic portfolio: Begin organizing your portfolio after completing your first semester of studies.

Initiate an SWRP: Organize and prepare your SWRP to set course of academic action and manage your time.

Start a social network: Create a file on the people who might help you and others with career challenges.

Perform internships: Participate in as many internships and community service work experiences as practical.

Informal interviews: Get comfortable with and make use of the informal interview, a seldom-used tool by students.

Join campus organizations: Join at least two campus-based organizations by the second semester of year one. Belong to at least four or five organizations and/or clubs by the time you graduate.

Join professional groups: Seek membership in professional groups and career-related societies.

Do practice interviews: Schedule live interviews as well as practice mock interviews with classmates.

Attend career prep events: Attend college job fairs as practical; take the opportunity to build your power network, and maybe get your resume critiqued.

Make a habit of reviewing and modifying your resume: Throughout the college experience, students should review, update, and modify their resumes after each semester. Make it a point to incorporate new information every semester.

Prepare biographical statement: Develop a biographical statement to highlight your academic history and work experience.

Join your national and local alumni associations: Make joining your national and local alumni associations priority one; they are repositories of tremendous network capital.

Form peer-learning groups: Participate in or start a peer-learning group. It looks good on a resume and is a powerful way to experience teamwork.

Seek reference letters and commendations: Make an effort to seek support letters on the way to graduation. These letters will prove to be useful in your job search and in preparing for interviews.

Develop job list: Use informal interviews, your professional affiliations, faculty engagement, and peers to compile a potential job list.

Mine social network: Devote attention to mining your social network—that is, look at the associations, talents, and the assets that empower other students, as well as making the network entirely about you.

Prepare job search resume: Prepare a door-opening one- or two-page resume that opens doors to the interview table.

Draft resume cover letter: Have in your possession a boiler plate cover letter that you tweak when needed.

Proof all written materials: Make a habit of proofreading materials and documents sent to prospective employers.

Initiate your job search in the junior year: If you have followed the lessons and instructions in this handbook, you're now equipped and ready to initiate a job research.

Author's Final Thoughts

> Think of yourself as on the threshold of unparalleled
> success. A whole clear, glorious life lies before you.
> Achieve! Achieve!
> —Andrew Carnegie

Writing the *Mentoring Handbook* was an exhilarating and challenging endeavour, and finishing it was a great sense of accomplishment. However, in the three-plus years spent writing the handbook, there were times when I questioned the noteworthiness of such a book. Would it impact the mind-sets of students as I imagined? And would it motivate students to take personal responsibility for learning? Moreover, I wondered if the handbook truly offered a fresh conversation on college readiness.

A key to helping students maximize the college experience, I believed, was to start a new conversation on postsecondary learning expectations. The conversation had to go beyond merely telling students to be sure to study, get good grades, and graduate. And don't disappoint us; the family is expecting to see you graduate this spring.

As the paragraphs and pages unfolded over those three long years of writing, my doubts lingered, but my confidence grow as well. Writing my final thoughts to close out this literary piece, I take a measure of comfort in knowing that students won't look at college the same way again after reading *The College Mentoring Handbook: The Way of the Self-Directed Learner*. By reading the handbook, they will realize that succeeding in college is by and large a management issue. Applying the strategies and guidance provided students will help them make better choices in the way they handle learning, and subsequently blueprint career pathways. In particular, it is my hope that the *Mentoring Handbook* serves to empower first-generation students to unlock their potential and develop the skill sets needed to compete and prosper in the global community.

**Go forth with confidence
and follow the direction
you set for yourself.
—Henry David Thoreau**

Notes

Notes

Printed in the United States
By Bookmasters